OCCUPY WOMEN

OCCUPY WOMEN

A Manifesto for Positive Change in a World Run by Men

Maureen F. Fitzgerald, PhD

(CP)

CENTERPOINT MEDIA

For information:
CenterPoint Media
www.CenterPointInc.com

LIBRARY AND ARCHIVES CANADA CATALOGUING IN PUBLICATION
Fitzgerald, Maureen F., author
    Occupy women : a manifesto for positive change in a world run by men / Maureen F. Fitzgerald.

Includes bibliographical references.
Issued in print and electronic formats.

ISBN 978-0-9939840-8-2 (paperback)
ISBN 978-1-988072-08-1 (ebook)

    1. Feminism. 2. Women--Social conditions--21st century. 3. Male domination (Social structure). I. Title.

HQ1236.F58 2016   305.42   C2015-905721-3
                                         C2015-905722-1

Edited by: Nance Fleming and Catherine Leek
Layout and design: Maureen Cutajar, Go Published
Cover design: Christine Unterthiner, Pilot Brands
Cover photo: www.Phototobinphotography.com
Cover Image: Part of image created by Gregor Črešnar, the Noun Project

"We are not here to hurt or defeat anyone
but to reveal the injustice that exists in the situation."
~ Rabia Roberts

Contents

Preface

Occupy Women is the most important book I have ever written.

This book began about 10 years ago as I was writing a book for my daughters. That book, titled *Gritty Is the New Pretty,* is all about helping girls develop resilience, courage and self-esteem. But as I was writing I kept getting this deep nagging feeling that something was missing. Looking back I am surprised it did not hit me sooner, particularly given that I am a lawyer and an expert on gender equality!

In any event the big light that went on in my head was this: Even if I raise my daughters to be confident and courageous, they will still have to fight off a whole society that sexualizes and degrades them. At that point, I changed the direction of my writing and proceeded to write three books on the barriers that women face and that hold women back. This book is the third in that series. The first is on corporate barriers (*Lean Out*) the second is on motherhood barriers (*Motherhood is Madness*) and this book, *Occupy Women*, is on society-wide barriers.

In my initial research for this book I asked myself many questions. They ultimately became my Contents because, as it turned out, these provide a quick summary of the ways in which we hold women back. Although there are undoubtedly more barriers, these seem to arise most frequently. Here are some of my original questions.

Why do we as a society:

- Value masculine traits more than feminine traits?

- Devalue roles that females tend to occupy, like nursing?

- Stereotype women, particularly wives and mothers?

- Pressure women to be beautiful, sexy and nice to everyone?

- Exclude women from law-making and governance?

- Pay women less than men for similar work?

- Tolerate the abuse and rape of women?

- Use language that excludes women?

- Allow millions of women to live in poverty?

- Accept pornography and the sex-trade of girls?

- Rarely see women in or behind the news and other media?

- Sexualize young girls and criticize powerful women?

- Discriminate against women just because they are female?

- Devalue emotions, intuition and other feminine strengths?

- Make it difficult for women to gain high positions in corporations and government?

In *Occupy Women* I provide answers to all of these questions and, indeed, the chapters of my book map loosely onto these particular questions.

As you read *Occupy Women* you will begin to see how many of our institutions and biases work together to hold women back. You will also learn (in the form of 21 strategies) how to dismantle this system and build a new one that is good for women and the whole world.

Introduction

"The blunt truth is that men still run the world. .... When the suffragettes marched in the streets, they envisioned a world where men and women would truly be equal. A century later, we are still squinting, trying to bring that vision into focus." ~ Sheryl Sandberg

Have you ever wondered why women worldwide suffer so much poverty and violence and why so few are in powerful positions of influence? Why are so many women poor and why are so few at the top of corporations or government? More importantly, why have women barely advanced in the world over the last century and why in many ways have they slipped backward?

Many of us like to think that women's struggles are mostly historic and that it's just a matter of time before things dramatically improve for women. We think of rape and violence as a personal problem between individual men and women. When women are kept prisoners in their homes we think it's just a handful of machismo fathers (from a particular cultural or religious background) who are trying to protect their wives and daughters from potential harm (usually from other men).

We also think that if we teach women how to grow food they will benefit from increased food production and avoid poverty. We believe that when girls and women gain more access to education they will eventually be able to take charge of their lives. We assume that female graduates will move organically into the highest positions in corporations and government and will work alongside men, creating laws that benefit everyone.

But this has not happened and many of these explanations are simply not true. They most definitely do not provide the whole picture. In fact, such observation provides a distorted view of what is really going on. Indeed, this reasoning actually masks the deepest causes of women's suffering and slow progress.

The truth is this: Many if not all of "women's problems" today are not historic, temporary, individual, cultural or even religious. Most are universal problems experienced by all women. Although we like to think the injustices and hurdles faced by women are relatively small and suffered only by a few, most issues of inequality and injustice affect all women and are in some way related to a much larger problem and that problem is quite simply a lack of female empowerment. This want of power exists and persists because we live within an outdated societal structure that keeps women down.

We humans have lived on this planet for almost 4 million years and yet it has only been in the last 3,000 years that men and women have not lived as equals. Indeed, archeological evidence suggests that about 10,000 years ago women were not only worshipped as goddesses, but held a somewhat higher status and were more respected than men.

We currently live in societies where small groups of men are in control of politics, money, media and power. They retain their control by maintaining a gender bias and keeping women out of power. Although this may sound somewhat sinister, I do not ever think of this as a problem solely having to do with men. Rather, I see this as a dilemma with our whole "operating system." This system has been researched by many academics and has apparently been evolving over thousands of years. It is a system that was essentially designed by men for the benefit of men.

So here's the question I want to ask: Who gave men all this power? Who built the political system, the economic system and the corporate laws that allow our hierarchal institutions to flourish? How did we as a society come to think that this type of societal organization is the best or only way to function? More importantly, why can't we see what is really going on?

Many years ago, the legal scholar, Catherine McKinnon, used the metaphor of a playground to examine this quandary. She asked women why they would want to play in a playground where the slide is so massive that women can't even step up onto the first rung of its ladder. Or why we would want to play on the swings that are so high that when we get pushed off we break our legs. She suggested that it might be easier for women to build a whole new playground rather than to try to play in or rebuild the one that's been built for men.

But changing it seems so daunting, as author Ken Dolan-Del Vecchio explains:

> One reason for our complacency is that the roots of inequality within our society have grown deep, strong and validated by law. Europeans brought with them to this land a hierarchal system of wealth and property ownership that was the forebear of our current economic and political order. Within that system, hierarchies based upon class, gender, race, and sexual orientation were mandated by law.

Essentially, we can't blame women for inaction. Not only is the problem invisible but most women do not have a moment to spare. Nor do they have access to information or practical advice on how to easily dismantle a patriarchy! Indeed, the type of research-based information contained in this book took me almost 10 years to find, read, understand and synthesize.

I personally think that if we are able to shift our societal operating system so that it better reflects and represents women, we can build a better world with men and women as full partners.

So what shall we do?

- First, we must admit that women in the world today are held back and suffer in ways that men do not. We must recognize that it's not the fault of men or women, but rather the system that is designed to favor men. We must acknowledge women's reality and see the link between "women's problems" (such a violence, poverty and discrimination) and our society-wide "operating system."

- Second, we must look at the various parts of this system and notice how they work together to keep women down. We must investigate our personal *beliefs* as well as the *institutions* we built upon these beliefs together with the *tools* we use to reinforce this system – just as an anthropologist would if examining an ancient society.

- Third, we must take action and build a better society – men and women together as partners.

As you read this book will begin to see how our institutions and biases work together to maintain the status quo and exactly how women are held back, not by particularly evil people, but by our whole societal system. You will also learn (in the form of 21 strategies) how to dismantle and re-build a new system that is not just good for women, but for the world.

A Note About Occupy Women

I am not the first woman to write about how women in the world are held back by our whole society. Nor am I the first to talk openly about our patriarchal roots and our male-favoring institutions. But what I have done here is explain these concepts in a straightforward and practical way. My aim is to quickly educate women so they can both understand what is really going on and take action (without having to read several 300-page academic books).

In this book I do three things.

- I acknowledge women's reality and shine a light on the link between "women's problems" and our patriarchal system. I refuse to blame men or women and instead blame the system.

- I describe the problems that we can see (such as poverty and discrimination) and also the relationships to the deeper roots of the problems. These include our *beliefs* about women, our *institutions* (such as our corporations) and our *tools* of implementation (such as the media and religions).

- I provide specific action steps that both men and women can take to bring about positive and long-lasting change.

In writing this book, I hope to stimulate a movement – Occupy Women.

I want to remind all women that they are perfect just as they are and that although they are currently being treated poorly and unfairly in our society, as human beings, they deserve so much more and in my humble opinion are never secondary.

Please join me in this Occupy Women Movement. As actor Emma Watson so eloquently said in her famous 2014 speech to the United Nations (launching the UN-based movement "HeforShe"): "If not me, then who? If not now, then when?"

Part One

The Hidden Secret

Chapter 1

Acknowledge Our Thousand-Year-Old Hierarchy

"The damage of a patriarchal system not only comes from having men at the top, but also because in doing so, we devalue and push down everything below men to maintain the system. Dominance and control are sadly used to keep the system in place. The world is currently set up according to masculine models of thought and structure, and it has been for thousands of years. Aggression, force, domination and control have been at the heart of our social agreements. Organization, technology and rational analysis have been the order of this very long day." ~ Marianne Williamson

Nicholas Kristof and Sheryl WuDunn created a world-wide movement to advance women around the world. In their best-selling book, *Half the Sky*, they describe the disturbing reality of women around the globe. Millions of women, even in North America, are kept as slaves in their own homes, being paid almost nothing for their work and being held back from educational and medical services – simply because they are female.

There are many books describing the plight of women in the world. There are also hundreds of academic texts and articles describing the causes of these problems and the reasons women are barely advancing in terms of status and power. All of them say pretty much the same thing: women are not advancing and there is one main reason why.

Professor Stephanie Vermeulen, in her book *Stitched-Up,* paints a distressing picture in a handful of statistics:

- 70% of the 1.3 billion people who live on less than $1 a day are women.

- The selling of girls and women earns human traffickers $7 billion annually.

- 700,000 women are raped annually in the US.

- Over 50% of the people murdered in India in 1995 were wives murdered by their husbands.

As for women's advancement in the corporate and business world, here is an excerpt from my recent book *Lean Out:*

Every year corporations and academics gather data and statistics about women's advancement. Year after year, the research shows that women are barely advancing at work and in business and in some cases are slipping back. Women hold significantly fewer numbers of powerful positions in corporations and government. Women are less likely than men to be considered for promotions and high-level positions. Women also earn less than men, are promoted less and have fewer mentors.

Here are a few recent statistics of women in various occupations in the United States from the article, "The Women's Leadership Gap" (August 4, 2015) by the Center for American Progress (www.americanprogress.org):

- Doctors: 35.5%
- Movie directors of top 250 films: 17%
- US House of Representatives: 19.4%
- CEOs in S&P 500 US corporations: 4.6%
- College professors (full):   30%

In her best-selling book *Lean In,* Sheryl Sandberg, Facebook COO, recounts the depressing statistics about women falling off corporate ladders and lists the specific obstacles women face including, "blatant and subtle sexism, discrimination and sexual harassment. Too few workplaces offer the flexibility and access to child care and parental leave that are necessary for pursuing a career while raising children. Men have an easier time finding mentors and sponsors who are invaluable for career progression. Plus women have to prove themselves to a far greater extent than men do."

These books and others not only describe "women's problems" but also the reasons for these problems. And here is what they conclude: At the root of women's problems lies a hidden secret. The one thing that these women share is that they live within a type of society that was built by men for the benefit of men. This type of society is called a patriarchy and has evolved over thousands of years.

In 1981 psychologist Anne Wilson Schaef wrote an international bestseller, *Women's Reality,* shining a clear light on this patriarchal system. She defines it as a society-wide operating system that she calls a "White Male System" (WMS) because it has predominantly been influenced by white males over thousands of years and white males continue to hold the majority of power in our society.

One of the most important aspects of this system is that women are seen to be inferior to males. According to Schaef, "To be born female means to be born innately inferior, damaged, that there is something inherently wrong with us." Schaef calls it the "original sin" of being born female because it is the birthright of women and that can never change, unless, of course, we change the system.

Within this system, women also lack power. Indeed this lack of power and lower status is every female's biggest issue. It is central to all our so-called "female problems," as beautifully described here by one of my favorite authors, Selma Greenberg:

> In all cases feminists believe that the hard core of sexism is the unequal access to power and the use and misuse of power between

women and men. ... Feminists believe that women's troubles are not usually the suggested ones: premenstrual cramps, postpartum depression, and hot flashes. Women's trouble is basically our trouble. They remain second class in a world where they have never been first class.

As explained by Adrienne Rich in her famous book, *Of Woman Born*, "A male-based system is nothing more than a familial-social, ideological, political system in which men – by force, direct pressure, or through ritual, tradition, law, and language, customs, etiquette, education, and the division of labor, determine what part women shall or shall not play, and in which the female is everywhere subsumed under the male."

According to Schaef this system, "Controls almost every aspect of our culture. It makes our laws, runs our economy, sets our salaries, and decides when and if we go to war or remain at home. It decides what knowledge is and how it is to be taught. Like any system it has both positive and negative aspects but because it is only a system it can be clarified, examined and changed within and without."

Indeed Schaef discovered something quite remarkable. This entire societal operating system is based almost entirely on two ideas. The first is that everything in the world is one big hierarchy and the second is that the use of dominance is considered the best way to run the world. These two ideas, which are reinforced by the myth of "survival of the fittest" underlie our entire society and are seen as the guiding principles by which we can best control citizens, allocate resources and organize society.

In this big hierarchy, God (a man) is placed at the top, followed by men, then women, children, animals, plants and minerals, in that order. Men are most important (next to God) and everything else below men is valued less. Although this hierarchal "worldview" is really only a theory about how we humans can best function on earth (and thankfully it is slowly changing) the roots are obviously still firmly in place and are wreaking havoc.

Best-selling author Sue Monk Kidd describes how she untangled her deeply Christian beliefs that were intractably linked to patriarchal beliefs and draws particular attention to the fact that these beliefs are almost set in stone. She noticed that they have slowly become embedded in the human psyche, been passed on as the natural and "divinely created" order of life, and thus have become our way of life in Western civilization.

The concept of hierarchy and domination was re-visited by Riane Eisler in her books, *The Chalice and the Blade* and *The Power of Partnership*. Similar to Schaef, Eisler describes our current worldview and societal operating system as a dominance-based model. She compares this to a partnership-based paradigm wherein men and women could share power equally.

According to Eisler our dominance model has four key aspects to it. First, it is based on authoritarianism or "strong-man" rule. Second, it subscribes to male dominance where one half of the population is ranked over the other. Third, it accepts violence as necessary, from wife beating to war. And finally, it views dominator relations as inevitable and even moral, thus tolerating killing, enslaving and torturing those who are "inferior."

In this hierarchy, where women are second-class citizens, there are patterns of behavior that impact not just women but husband-wife and all other relationships, including mother and child. Greenberg describes how this hierarchy plays out in our families through an example from a Psychology 101 textbook: "The boss yells at his employee, who stands there and takes it. When the employee returns home that evening, he yells at his wife, who stands there and takes it. When the wife catches sight of her children, she yells at them. They stand there and take it. Finally, the children turn on the household pet, which stands there and takes it."

In this hierarchy, males are seen as having more value and so, too, are male attributes and traits. By observing thousands of cultural messages, Schaef was able to discern these values and labeled them "male values." In the chart below she compares them to those she defines as "female values."

Male Values	Female Values
One-upmanship	Equal peers
Zero sum and Win/Lose	Abundance and Win/Win
Individual focus	Relationship focus
Lead out front	Facilitate contributions
Direct and linear	Multi-dimensional
Logical	Intuitive and Multi-dimensional
Communicate to win	Communicate to bridge and clarify needs
Blame and accountability	Responsibility and action
Results and outcomes	Process
Strict rules	Consensual guidelines

In other words, to quote Monk Kidd, "It seem[s] clear that patriarchy has valued rationality, independence, competitiveness, efficiency, stoicism, mechanical forms and militarism – things traditionally associated with the 'masculine.' Less valued are being, feeling, art, listening, intuition, nurturing and attachment – things traditionally associated with the 'feminine'."

These differences were also discovered by linguist Deborah Tannen in her research on how men and women communicate differently. In her book, *You Just Don't Understand,* Dr. Tannen explains that the reason men and women get into so many disputes is because men tend to see the world as hierarchal and women tend to see the world as connected.

She discovered, for example, that in conversations, men are more inclined to boast and play one-upmanship whereas women are more inclined to downplay their expertise in an attempt to include others. Men value winning and saving face as all important, whereas women do not. This fundamental difference really helped me to understand male-female conflict and communication and provided me with a whole new way of seeing how males and females view the world as collaborative and competitive.

A harsher perspective of patriarchy has been taken by many academics who see the subjugation of women as sinister. Vermeulen suggests that centuries ago powerful males abused their power by taking,

> [W]hat was sacred in a woman and demonising it, or turning power-ful female attributes such as our potent sexuality into a source of great shame. One of the most coercive methods that men used in biblical times was to appoint the Almighty as their spokesman. This is how the Jewish, Christian and Islamic view of women metamor-phosed into God's judgement, providing myths such as females being the source of all evil and the first woman being created from the rib of Adam.

All of our institutions, such as our economic, legal and even our ed-ucational institutions, were built within this system and it is reflected in all sorts of ways from boardrooms to bedrooms. Yet one example of these hierarchies crumbling is the modern corporation that is slowly moving from a top-down, command and control model of leadership to a shared or collaborative leadership system. Indeed, leadership expert Peter Senge predicted in 1997 that the old-fashioned control model of leadership would not survive in the 21st century (although it has!).

As a final note, it is important to avoid the trap of confusing patriar-chy with matriarchy. Matriarchy is not patriarchy with a different sex. As Rich says, matriarchy is a society where "female creative power is pervasive and women have organic authority, rather than one in which women establish dominance and control over the man, as the man over women in a patriarchy."

Unfortunately the word "patriarchy" has become so scary and danger-ous and has now become "the word that shall not be mentioned" (as in the Harry Potter stories). Thus it is important to restate my position. Men are not to blame. Our whole system is. It is a terrible shame and lie to suggest that discussions of patriarchy involve any type of man-hating. Any labeling of this sort should be viewed as a tool to silence women.

The Bottom Line. In North America we live within a patriarchal system of society that has evolved over thousands of years. It is a model of social governance that is reflected in our culture, politics, corporations and families. Although it is no longer considered the best way to allocate resources and keep order in society, it remains intact and holds many women back. Here are the essential components of this system:

- It assumes that the world and all its inhabitants exist in one big hierarchy.

- At the top of the hierarchy is a male god with men close behind.

- In this hierarchy women are below men in status and worth.

- Animals, plants and other living things fall at the bottom of the hierarchy.

- It assumes that only the fittest are meant to survive.

- It uses dominance to maintain control.

Because females are seen as second-class citizens under this system, they tend to be restricted from access to privilege, influence, status and power. Although it may be difficult to change, our patriarchal system is neither inevitable nor sustainable.

What To Do. The most important thing to do is to "un-shame" the word patriarchy so we can talk about patriarchy as a system. This avoids the defensiveness that can arise when men feel blamed or responsible. We must question everything about it, but particularly the idea that the entire planet is one big hierarchy as opposed to an organic, interconnected unit. We must question why we see men as most valuable in our society and why male-based values, such as competition and aggression, are the bedrock of this system. We must ask how we can create a system that embraces more feminine values, like collaboration and caring.

Chapter 2

Uncover Our Hidden Cultural Rules

"What customs and rituals do they observe? What kinds of women and men are respected in this culture? What kinds of body shapes are considered ideal? How are sex roles assigned? What are the sanctions for breaking rules?" ~ Mary Pipher

So how do you begin to tease apart our culture and a patriarchal system since so many of our cultural rules are invisible to the naked eye?

The easiest way to understand our culture or "operating system" and its impact is through the famous words of Marshall McLuhan who described culture as similar to the water in a fish tank. Although the fish do not know they are in water, it is all around them and supports their life. Culture is like the air we breathe.

Our culture consists of laws written down in big books, economic procedures and processes, corporate polices and guidelines and family rules. It also consists of customs, traditions, taboos and biases that are passed on from generation to generation. In combination we refer to this glue as our cultural rules – and many are holding women back.

There are two types of cultural rules directed at women. First are those that tell women what they can do or the role they should play in society. These include pressure to stay within certain "feminine" jobs or careers, particularly mothers and wives. The other type of rules tell women how they should act. These include pressure to be nice and sexy among others. Women and girls are bombarded daily with clear instructions about how to behave. We are told to be super workers, super moms and super wives. Millions of hidden rules tell us in very clear terms how we are to behave as females in our communities and in our homes. But no matter the type, the cultural rules that harm women most are those that limit their freedom and choices.

One of the most important things to understand about these cultural rules is that they are rarely designed by women. They evolved over thousands of years by societies where men held the majority of influence and power. Most were created without the input of women (or children) and most were designed primarily for the benefit of those in power, who at that time were mostly men.

This is why for most of our history women were not allowed to go to university or participate in politics. For centuries women were not allowed to take on paid work and were considered the property of their fathers or husbands. Women were not permitted to become church ministers, hold elected offices or vote.

Since the majority of our modern religions were established by men, it should come as no surprise that only men sat with Jesus at the last supper or that many women are not permitted to enter places of worship or, if they did, must cover their heads by way of subservience. Indeed in many modern religions women remain inferior in men's eyes and are told they are inferior "in god's eyes" and are therefore not permitted to take on leadership roles.

In her book, *Toward a New Psychology of Women*, Jean Baker Miller explains how these cultural rules are created. At various points in time rules are made by the dominant group in society. This group, like our modern government, sets specific rules and expectations about how people can and should behave in society. These rules are based on this dominant group's ideas about what suits the society in which they live.

These rules do not only consist of laws; they consist of the tools to implement and enforce these laws. Slavery is a perfect example. We as a society created laws that made the ownership of blacks by whites legal and we enforced these laws through the police and the courts. We also prevented kind-hearted individuals from helping blacks by arresting them, terrorizing them and shaming them. In essence, our entire culture prevented blacks from being free by accepting these rules as cultural norms. That is why slavery was so difficult to overcome, and why, to this day, racist attitudes towards blacks still persists. To my mind, one of the best books (as well as one of the best movies) in Western culture on the topic of racism is Harper Lee's, *To Kill a Mockingbird* (still one of my favorites).

When dismantling the culture it is useful to see our operating system as having three distinct parts:

1. Our set of beliefs and values (e.g., what women can and should do).

2. Our institutions that are built upon these beliefs (e.g., our financial and corporate institutions, etc.).

3. Our tools used to implement, promote and reinforce these beliefs and institutions (e.g., religion, media, customs and rituals, etc.).

Here's a model that shows how each of these three parts impacts the lives of women.

The System: How Beliefs, Institutions and Tools Impact Women

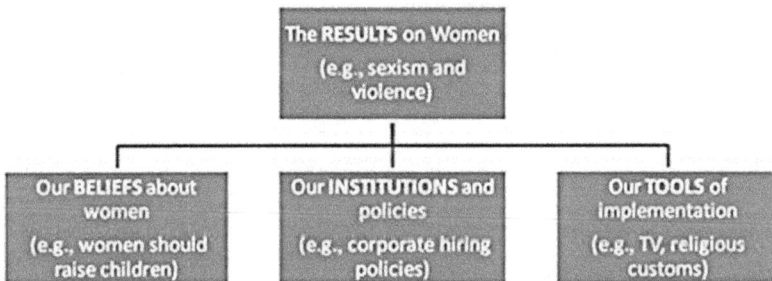

The RESULTS on Women (e.g., sexism and violence)

| Our BELIEFS about women (e.g., women should raise children) | Our INSTITUTIONS and policies (e.g., corporate hiring policies) | Our TOOLS of implementation (e.g., TV, religious customs) |

If we want enduring change, we need to work on all three of these parts at the same time. For example, if we adopt the belief that mothers can both work *and* care for their children and we shift corporate systems so that people can work flexible hours, then women would be more likely to have careers. As for tools, however, unless we convince the media to stop portraying mothers as disheveled and torn, as they so often do, women will still feel held back. If you change just one aspect, say a shift in your corporate system to promote more women, but fail to address underlying beliefs, such as women are poor leaders, change will be very slow.

Although our systems and tools shift over time, our attitudes and mind-sets tend to lag behind. This is because they are often not challenged. Indeed because they exist in our heads and are so deeply engrained and intricately interwoven, we're barely even aware that our mind-sets exist. Much like those parents who do not question their parenting style until they see the negative results in their child's behavior, we do not question our beliefs until they cause some sort of discomfort. At the same time, these beliefs are usually passed along from generation to generation buried within traditions and customs that, if challenged, would be considered sacrilege.

The Bottom Line. Our system, which consists of beliefs, institutions and tools of implementation, holds women back. Our outdated *beliefs* about what women can and should do in society are out of step with women's progress and are very resilient to change. Our *institutions* (such as our corporate and economic institutions), which are built upon these beliefs, rarely change unless under severe pressure. The *tools* we use to implement and reinforce our beliefs, such as television shows, work as powerful propaganda. Working together, these three parts of our culture prevent women from being truly powerful or free. Most problematic are our outdated beliefs, not only because they are invisible, but because they are deeply embedded and accepted as the status quo.

What To Do. We need to notice our whole system consisting of powerful and mostly invisible rules that impact all of us. We need to look closely at the diagram above and identify all of the beliefs, systems and tools that are causing women all sorts of problems. From our assumptions about the role of women in society to our corporate policies and even the magazines in our living rooms — all contribute to holding women back in some way. By looking at the parts of the system we can also begin to see how we can leverage change — whether in our homes, at our jobs or in the community. As Pipher says, we need to observe our own culture with the eyes of an anthropologist in a strange new society. The rest of this book is dedicated to this task.

Chapter 3

Challenge Male Privilege

"Even by that age (8) I knew unquestioningly how important and powerful it was to be a male. I was also learning how important and powerful it was to be white. In school I was told that white men were the thinkers and doers who made civilization happen. All of my history, science and mathematics and storybooks made that clear as did a look at any of the television programs, newspapers or magazines that were available to me. Being 'all boy' and white meant I was in the very best club." ~ Ken Dolan-Del Vecchio

One key aspect of a patriarchal system is the belief that males are intrinsically more valuable than females. Growing up Catholic, I learned from a very young age that, as a female, I was a second-class citizen and that my entire role in life was to serve a male God. I was told that only men could be the heads of households, priests or popes. As a girl, I had to wear a hat in church because females were not worthy of receiving God directly.

Although modern thinkers find this idea of male supremacy offensive, this fundamental belief still lingers in the minds of billions of people around the world, and even in our homes. In fact, this thought continues to permeate all of our society and its institutions. And although almost completely unconscious, this single belief is the root cause of most of women's problems today. If I were given the power to remove just one belief from our millions of beliefs, this would be my choice.

The belief that men are more valuable and deserving than women is called "male privilege." It assumes that males are better than females simply because of their sex. They are more able to be leaders and more deserving of the world's wealth and opportunities. They are more powerful, more intelligent and more valuable to society and the world. This idea assumes men deserve to be the leaders. It is the root cause of all discrimination and sexism against women.

From the day we are born we are inundated with society's messages regarding our role as female and the limits begin. Though it seems innocent enough, we hear things like, "She's so sweet." "He's so strong." "She's pretty." "He's smart." "She'll make a wonderful mother." "He might be the next president!" We are reared by way of expressions and expectations such as these to accept a secondary role.

Because males are born privileged, we give to them quite undeserved deference without question. To help uncover your bias, you might ask yourself these questions.

- Who usually gets to stay out latest, teen boys or teen girls?

- Who often speaks loudest in classrooms, boys or girls?

- Who is expected to be the corporate or political leaders, boys or girls?

- Who is expected to help cook family meals and do domestic chores, boys or girls?

- Who is expected to go on to earn a big income, boys or girls?

This is the type of insidious favoritism in our society that not only sets boys up for thinking that they deserve this special treatment but also encourages them to believe that girls are subservient to them. Yet because this bias is so engrained and invisible, it is very difficult to see, and even more difficult to correct. In fact, most men have no idea what women are talking about when they talk about equality or equal opportunity. They think everything is fair.

This is the way privilege tends to work for those who are privileged. In fact, research shows that those who are in a position of power find it quite difficult to understand those without power and their struggles. In his book *Making Love, Playing Power*, psychologist Ken Dolan-Del Vecchio describes the power structure this way: "It's not difficult to look upward into the power hierarchy and see what others are receiving, but we're not. It's often very uncomfortable, however, to look downward to see our advantages over others. Recognizing this privilege, however, is a key starting point for men who want to make important positive changes in their relationships."

Until very recently, "the male" was considered the norm or "standard" in all of our sciences. Indeed almost all research was conducted on males, from baboons to humans. For centuries scientists considered males as the "standard" and compared everything else to them. This bias was slowly uncovered by critical thinkers when their theories did not seem to make sense when applied to women. One of the first recognitions of this bias was revealed in the work of early anthropologists, such as Margaret Mead. Even though she was a woman, Mead's original research on gorillas suggested that the norm was the male gorilla and the females were described in relation to males.

More recently, sociologist Carol Gilligan discovered in her research that males and females make very different moral decisions, and found that women as a group responded quite differently than men to ethical issues. Prior to Gilligan, all research on morals was conducted on males and findings were automatically extended to females. Gilligan single-handedly shook the entire academic world by introducing the idea that the theories and models we developed over hundreds of years (based solely on males) were wrong. (Simone de Beauvoir, author of the book *The Second Sex*, describes this uber-focus on males in detail and is well worth the read.)

Dolan-Del Vecchio suggests that the main problem in relationships is the imbalance and misuse of power. He suggests that men suffer from an attitude of "male entitlement" and this wreaks havoc on relationships as well as the less entitled partner. He defines entitlement as: "[T]he pattern in which we men prioritize and enact our thoughts, feelings and desires without adequately consulting or even considering the implications for those closest to us, and, in most cases, without even noticing that we are behaving in this fashion. In other words, it is blind disregard for the inconsiderate nature of our pattern of choices."

Dolan-Del Vecchio suggests that these habits generally go unnoticed because they're widely accepted as the natural order of things. We accept these relationship patterns without question. Here are his examples of how entitlement shows up in relationships.

- Delegating to one's partner (usually by default) responsibilities for maintaining social connections.

- Refusing to gain competence with housework and infant care.

- Unself-consciously prioritizing one's own feelings and desires over those of one's partner and other family members.

- Claiming the right to make far-reaching decisions on behalf of other people without even consulting them.

- Forgetting about one's partner's distress or other strong feelings even when they were expressed recently.

The Bottom Line. Without realizing it, we as a society favor men. This bias, called male privilege, has been passed down through generations. It assumes that men are not only more valuable in society but also more deserving. Boys are granted this from the day they are born and girls are cast as secondary to males and often subservient to them. We unconsciously grant boys and men privileges simply because they are male.

What To Do. We must dismantle the whole idea of male privilege. We must surface the absurd belief that males are somehow better and stop thinking that men are more deserving than women. We must look closely at how we treat boys and girls differently and ask why we do this. We must notice every time privilege raises its head, particularly in husband-wife relationships and we must teach men how their sense of self-importance is wreaking havoc on women, on relationships and in the world.

Chapter 4

Balance Masculine and Feminine

"During this time [of patriarchy], the feminine principles of nonviolence and surrender and the values of intuition, nurturing and healing were pushed aside. We forget the power of the tender touch. Slowly but surely, generation after generation, over thousands of years it was made to seem ridiculous. She was debased in men as well as in women, all of us risking shame when choosing to relate to her...She was silenced, just invalidated. She could still speak, but she wouldn't be heard." ~ Marianne Williamson

Linked closely to the idea of male superiority is our societal belief that males and the masculine are correct and good and that females and the feminine are bad and secondary. Male attributes and skills are seen to be most valuable and their perspectives are most accurate. Females are generally considered abnormal with behaviors, attributes and strengths that are not quite as good. Here are some examples of our societal beliefs.

- Tall is good; short is bad.

- Tough is good; tender is weak.

- Firm is good; kind is secondary.

- Loud is good; soft spoken is bad.

- Deep voices command authority; high pitched voices do not.

In other words, the male is correct and the female "is less than correct." Females are seen to be different, odd, inconsistent – an aberration. As Freud labelled it, the female is a penis-less male.

The myth of women simply being a "version" of men is promoted in the biblical creation story of Adam and Eve. Eve is said to have been born from a rib taken from Adam. It is said that he came first, Eve second, with the idea that she came "from him." Here are some of the erroneous assumptions that have been made and continue to be made about girls and women that emerge from following this way of thinking.

- Females are the weaker sex.

- Women and girls need protection (from males).

- Females are better at helping others (e.g., child-rearing).

- Women are better at cleaning and cooking.

- Women are not very strong – physically or emotionally.

- Females are flighty, confused and unfocused.

- Women struggle with complex issues.

Not only do we, as a society, think that females are weaker and somehow inferior, we also de-value their intelligences and attributes, including such things as nurturing and intuition.

If you think that you no longer harbor any of these outdated beliefs, I urge you to answer the following questions to help you uncover your own hidden beliefs about females and femininity. Please answer both sets of questions in order.

- Girls are gentler than boys: True/False

- Girls are neater than boys: True/False

- Girls are more attractive than boys: True/False

- Girls cry more often than boys: True/False

- Girls are more caring than boys: True/False

- Girls are more afraid than boys: True/False

- Girls are less athletic than boys: True/False

- Girls are less assertive than boys: True/False

- Girls are less competitive than boys: True/False

Now answer these questions:

- Girls should be gentler than boys: True/False

- Girls should be neater than boys: True/False

- Girls should be more attractive than boys: True/False

- Girls should cry more often than boys: True/False

- Girls should be more caring than boys: True/False

- Girls should be more afraid than boys: True/False

- Girls should be less athletic than boys: True/False

- Girls should be less assertive than boys: True/False

- Girls should be less competitive than boys: True/False

As you can see, many of us automatically assume that girls are gentle and sensitive. Then, to make matters worse, we subtly suggest that these things are somehow "weak" or problematic. At the same time, we attribute boys with being athletic and assertive and then suggest these attributes are "strong" or positive. In other words, after we define what is "feminine" we then proceed to devalue or demean it!

How often have we heard that our so-called "feminine" behaviors are inappropriate? At the top of this list is, of course, crying, or showing any heightened emotions, even excitement. The following is a series of directions spoken and unspoken, but directed at girls and women, the origins of which stem from an intolerance of feminine tendencies or traits. The first portion of demands begin early in the home, continues throughout schooling and permeates the workplace as well. The latter half is directed specifically to women in the workplace.

- Don't cry.

- Don't giggle.

- Don't be sad – smile!

- Be nice!

- Don't be so sensitive.

- Don't display family photos in the workplace.

- Don't decorate your office.

- Don't dress "sexy."

- Don't dress "manly."

- Don't ask too many questions.

- Leave your family issues at home.

To reinforce these notions that women are "weak" and such weakness is a failing, we propagate stories about weak women. One of the most famous stories in this vein is the biblical story of Adam and Eve. As noted above, Eve was made from man, and the basic premise is that not only was Eve weak and stupid (allowing herself to be manipulated by a snake of all things), but she was so gullible that she took a bite of an apple that resulted in a "curse" on humanity for all time.

(The fact that this action also lands her the accusatory label of "evil" is a point that will be touched upon later.) Indeed, most women in my generation learned that because of Eve, God has been punishing women for all of Christian history. He does this by making childbirth painful and making women submit to men. And to add insult to injury, Eve's only apparent feminine strength in the story, her sensuality, is used to manipulate Adam and lead to his demise. The shame that all Christian women are supposed to feel from this story is an undercurrent of Christianity that endures to this day.

If we keep our thoughts on biblical female role models here, we need only consider the next most significant woman in the Bible — Mary, the Virgin (with a capital "V") mother of God. She is portrayed as an almost completely silent virgin, very giving and adoring of her son. In almost all of her statues she is depicted with a downward gaze. Always reverent, she is a "pure" and passive mother figure whose only significant role is/was to give birth to her son, Jesus, a miraculous occurrence since she remained a virgin. This is the "on-a-pedestal" standard that Christian women are ideally expected to meet. And then, of course, there is Mary of Magdalene who has been labelled, in Christian religious belief, a prostitute. She is depicted as an evil temptress whose role is to continually tempt Jesus, although more recently some historical scholars suggest, for those who believe she was based on a living person, that she may have been a princess and actually married to Jesus.

Many well-known thinkers have suggested that this downplaying of feminine aspects and the devaluing of females is not only bad for women, but bad for our whole society and the earth. Sue Monk Kidd, Marianne Williamson and Joan Borysenko stand out as thought leaders suggesting that by abandoning "the feminine" we are, in effect, killing the planet. It only takes a bit of looking around to see how we still view dominance, aggression and war as strong and necessary versus how we view compromise and peacemaking as weak.

The Bottom Line. At some level, we as a society still believe that males are better than females and that masculine attributes are preferable to feminine. We see girls and women as physically and psychologically weaker and boys as stronger. We see masculine skills such as aggression and competitiveness as more valuable than feminine skills such as empathy and intuition. Through our stories and traditions we reinforce this myth, causing many of us to undervalue females and lower our expectations of girls and women.

What To Do. Each of us must stop thinking that somehow males are better than females, in any context. We must look at women as being just as valuable as men, girls just as valuable as boys. We must look at the feminine strengths that have been downplayed and even condemned by Christian bible stories and religious myths. We must challenge the belief that somehow females are secondary and must question why a God would have made half of all humans as inferior and subservient to the other. To hold women back in this way not only harms women, but holds us all back as an enlightened and equal society.

Chapter 5

Question the "Femininity Message"

"As I came to know my own Inner Patriarch and those of other women, a clear pattern emerged. I could see how our patriarchs keep us in an inferior position – if not at our work, then in our relationships. They make us distrust ourselves. Even more important was the discovery that they make us distrust other women as well. They trust and value men, and those traditionally male qualities, more than women and anything traditionally feminine. I saw again and again how the Inner Patriarch devalued us and what we did just because we were women." ~ Sidra Stone

Every girl learns from a very young age what it means to be female and feminine. You might recall the phrase, "sugar and spice and everything nice" describing how girls are to behave. Our pink blankets and clothing cued our parents and others to hold us gently and speak to us in soft voices. As we grew, we learned how to dress (in frills and lace for some, but always with an aim to be pretty for most), what to say (never critical) and what to avoid (yelling and hitting).

These expectations of females have been evolving over the last 3000 years and are rooted in outdated thinking. The current concept of "female" and "feminine" is particularly problematic for women because it has its roots in our historic definitions, in which women's role in society was defined almost exclusively in relation to and for the benefit of men. For example, to be "feminine" was to be supportive, helpful and obedient to men.

And it's not just men who hold these outdated ideas about women. Since it is a culture-wide belief, even women hold the same beliefs in their conscious or subconscious minds. In her book, *The Shadow King*, Sidra Stone describes these beliefs as an unconscious voice within both women and men with its origins and traditions dating back six millennia.

She labels this bundle of thoughts as our "Inner Patriarch" who holds very strong ideas and feelings about all women and all things womanly. Here is a sample of the thoughts she identified.

- An unmarried women is an unfulfilled women.

- A wife's job – no matter who she is – is first and foremost to take care of her husband.

- A women without a child has not fulfilled her destiny.

- Women should stop pretending to be men. They should stay at home and stop wanting more.

- She's a woman and she'll never amount to anything.

- It's too bad she was born a woman. If only she were a man she could use some of her brains.

- Women are bitchy and "nags" underneath. "I don't like them."

- Women's hormonal imbalances make them unfit for any serious work.

- Women are illogical and lack focus.

- Women are too emotional and always overreacting.

- Women are basically weaker than men.

- Women have poor judgment. "I'd never use a women doctor or lawyer."

- Once a woman is no longer attractive and good for sex, she is basically useless.

- A woman should have babies, that's what she's good for.

Although many of these might sound absurd to some, having been passed along through generations, many of these thoughts exist in the backs of our minds, in our "subconscious."

Academics refer to this bundle of rules that is passed along from generation to generation as the "femininity message." They are the subtle messages our society gives to girls and women about what it means to be feminine. They tell us that menstruation is "the curse" and that being intuitive is witch-like. These messages also define what girls can and cannot do. To act in a feminine way is a complicated task.

Yet these messages are unfortunately at the root of many of our female stereotypes and basis for why we hold females back (why we hold "ourselves" back). Stone discovered that we, as a society, define the feminine role as fitting within the following three very strict categories, rejecting women who do not fit.

- Bitches are women who are successful in the world of men. We do not tend to see them as fully functioning women. They are males dressed as women and we are often waiting for them to stop being frauds (and fall in love with a man).

- Mothers are women who accept the protection of men and stay in the home, out of public life. We view them as large-breasted and nurturing, but also weak. We expect them to love children and housework although it's obvious they are frustrated in such narrow roles.

- Sages are women who reject the voice of patriarchy and remove themselves from the game. These women include prostitutes and wise women crones. They are rejected by society and although seem free are not fully connected to the world.

By comparing these narrow definitions to our very broad societal definition of "masculine" we quickly get the sense of how limiting these roles are for women and how not one of these definitions casts women as powerful or fulfilled.

41

It's important to know, however, that the definition of "feminine," though influenced by the past, is still made up by each generation. We actually decide as a society what we want females to be, as reflected in "The Professions for Women," an essay by Virginia Wolfe.

> She was intensely sympathetic. She was immensely charming. She was utterly unselfish. She excelled in the difficult arts of the family life. She sacrificed herself daily. If there was a chicken she took the leg; if there was a draft, she sat in it – in short she was so constituted that she never had a mind or wish of her own, but preferred to sympathize always with the minds and wishes of others.... I did my best to kill her. My excuse, if I were to be had up in a court of law, would be that I acted in self-defense. Had I not killed her, she would have killed me. (in Monk Kidd)

Some western authors have suggested that the way in which the Bible was interpreted (long after Jesus died) has played, and continues to play, a pivotal role in keeping women down and limiting the concept of the feminine, as described here by Monk Kidd:

> The Bible is no stranger to patriarchy. It was written mostly if not entirely by men. It describes a succession of societies over a period of roughly 1200 years whose public life was dominated by men... It talks almost only about men.... As a prescriptive text, moreover, the Bible has been interpreted as justifying the subordination of women to men.... As a text it has been presumed by hundreds of millions of people to speak with authority, moreover the Bible has helped to enforce what it prescribes.

Consider the outright acknowledgement of the failings of biblical works and their negative impact on women made by former US President Jimmy Carter. In his book, *A Call to Action: Women, Religion, Violence and Power*, Carter calls upon world leaders to take action to end violence against women perpetrated in the name of religion. As he says, "Women and girls have been discriminated against for far too long in a twisted interpretation of the word of God."

The Bottom Line. Today in North America we cling to a narrow and outdated version of the concept of "femininity." Based on ancient mind-sets, we as a society still think that girls and women should be helpful, considerate and obedient. We also think that the primary "feminine" role is to support men and be useful and pleasing to men. This is why, even today, we define feminine women as agreeable, likeable and sexy (to men). This narrow definition of femininity is reinforced through powerful rituals, traditions, social media and, most of all, religious works such as the Bible. This attitude not only holds women back by suggesting they are less than they truly are, but also by limiting them to roles that are confining and much too small for their true potential.

What To Do. We need to look closely at our societal beliefs about being "feminine" and tackle each and every one. We must replace our outdated version of "feminine" as supportive and compliant with one that is strong, wise, independent and fully capable. We must reject those limiting roles often described in religious stories and played out in outdated traditions. Rituals are very powerful in perpetuating archaic ideas about women. Any message that tells women that being feminine is either wrong or "less than" masculine must be challenged.

Chapter 6

End the Media's Stereotyping

"You want your daughter to realize that the characters of soap operas are highly dysfunctional. They behave in ways that are almost exactly the opposite of the behavior of healthy rational people. To meet the dramatic requirements of the writers who must endlessly prolong the suspense, the characters make terrible, often ridiculous choices based in emotions unleavened with rational thought. Often they are the worst emotions: jealousy, greed, envy and paranoia." ~ Nicky Marone

"Both men and women are offended by obvious sex-role stereotypes of women in our culture. Many of us are outraged at the objectification of maids in their own homes, prostitutes, low paid pink-collar workers, and so on. But how many of us really stop to examine the unconscious cultural beliefs that dictate our own parenting behavior?" ~ Jeanne Elium & Don Elium

One of my favorite television commercials is quite sexist. It starts out showing a full screen headshot of a father and a son. They are looking at something that we cannot see and are tilting their heads from side to side as if looking at something weird or something they had never seen before. Both have deeply perplexed looks on their faces. The father then says, "It's very strange. I don't know what it is." The son adds, "Me neither. Maybe mom knows." The camera pans out, showing the mother standing directly behind them with an amused smile on her face. The camera then turns around to focus in on the thing that has caused such confusion – an empty toilet paper roll!

Although mothers find this very funny because it acknowledges their reality, some men, my husband for one, are insulted by this advertisement. Why? Because it stereotypes him and other men as lazy fathers who don't help around the house and are at a loss of what to do when something as simple as the toilet paper runs out. When he complained about this depiction of men, I simply said, "Welcome to my life!" And by this, I meant "welcome to gender stereotyping," it's directed at women all the time in a myriad of media formats.

Advertisers that create such ads are masters of messaging and skilled at leveraging stereotypes to promote products. When working for clients to sell a product, their basic job is to manipulate declarations and perpetuate stereotyping in order to play upon our conscious and subconscious beliefs. More often than not, the gender stereotyping is aimed at women. For example, think of all the commercials that promote laundry detergent and bathroom cleaners. Do you recall many, if any, men in these types of advertisements? The answer is very rarely.

Advertisers intentionally use female stereotyping in such ads to evoke an emotional response – either pleasure at having their life made easier and/or frustration over life's difficulties. Either way, they create the "tension" needed to grab your "attention." However, what gets lost in all the emotions and humor is the fact that the media, and by this I include not just ads, but television, movies, news, newspapers, radio and YouTube, have become *the* primary and most powerful way in which our culture's expectations are passed along. From constant Internet connection to your doctor's office magazines, the media barrage both shows *and* tells women how to behave.

Media messaging works because we humans watch and learn through imitation. From birth till death, we copy what we see. The media essentially shows us by repeated example what we "should" buy, how we "should" look, how we "should" act and what we "should" eat. It underscores what is appropriate and not appropriate; what is wrong and what is right. We even know when to speak and when to keep quiet; all by subtle and not so subtle example.

For instance, to use a marital storyline, if we watch a drama series and the TV husband repeatedly lies to his wife (and behaves oh so charming as he does), even though we may not accept lying as natural or "right," we will eventually begin to believe that dishonesty is not so very terrible after all. By constant repetition of messaging, we adjust our thought processes accordingly and begin to imitate certain behavior. And since we start doing this at a very young age (research shows that within the first days of life children can imitate behavior), we easily end up imitating behavior that is shown to us our entire lives.

Since the media is such a huge part of our lives now, this means that an endless parade of actors (in movies, TV, videos, evening news, reality shows, gaming and even documentaries) send messages to you and me on a daily basis. For women, these messages are most often about how we should behave and interact with each other (most particularly how we should behave with men), but they also provide very real examples of everything from how to dress to how to decorate our houses and which toilet products will make our life better.

You can't walk away from one single show without, in some way, being affected by a message. Simply watching behavior in a TV show causes us to "normalize" or begin to think that it is common and acceptable, whether it is in real life or not. Each and every television show conveys layers and layers of pre-constructed information and opinions to us. And since most of our learning is subconscious; we are often not even aware it is happening.

The media tool is also the thread that holds our society together so we don't all run in different directions. It is our common understanding of the world beyond our own personal limited experiences. We actually need it to survive as a global community. It is, without question, one of the most phenomenally powerful tools of control over the masses. Indeed it was the power of media propaganda that promoted apartheid in South Africa and brought about Nazi Germany. It has lead countries to war and has been very effective in its repeated messaging to keep women down.

In my opinion, much of our media is destructive for women, as it reinforces outdated stereotypes. It tells us that we must strive to be beautiful, sexy, subservient and useful to men, and perfect in every way. If we're not all of these things, then we're somehow flawed and as a result must be devalued. It also shows us, by way of warning, what happens to women who speak up a bit too loudly. They are considered bitches and are discarded and often labelled as feminists, which our society tends to interpret as man-haters.

This continuous diet of negative media-messaging has a profound psychological influence on all of us and directly impacts women and their self-esteem.

Take, for instance, sitcoms and so-called "reality" programs. These can be, and often are, particularly harmful in their depiction of women, though subtly so because they use humor to get away with negative depictions. Although we watch them for the humor, we are also drawn to them because the characters are much like us, with similar everyday problems and struggles.

If asked, we may never admit to behaving like the characters in these shows, but they are essentially our role models, providing us with responses and solutions to life events, however absurd. We know on one level that what we're watching is simply "make believe" and that it doesn't depict the way "real" people make choices in life, yet something still registers in our subconscious. A joke and laugh track with accompanying derogatory dialogue used in direct juxtaposition to a scene involving a strong-willed or exceptionally bright female character denotes disrespect and contempt; such a character is often literally referred to as a "bitch" at some point in the scene.

Or consider another repeated stereotype that we're fed unendingly: the "dumb blonde" character. There's always a demeaning joke to perpetuate the disrespect and suggest that if women have a certain color of hair, they're bound to be stupid. With regard to the latter stereotype, there's an interesting twist. While the blonde character is made fun of, she's very often considered a good mate for the male character. The idea that a dumb woman can be taken advantage of and controlled seems to be the undercurrent, though the notion of a trophy wife or girlfriend is also a ready interpretation. A steady diet of this type of messaging is not constructive on any level.

Here are a few facts about television:

- TV does not depict the way real people make choices in life.

- Reality shows do not have much resemblance to real life. There is little to no accountability for the characters.

- TV characters are actors and not real people, living real lives.

- TV sitcoms and dramas, and even newscasts, are filled with stereotypes about girls and women.

- TV programming contains an excessive amount of violence, inordinately directed at female victims.

Television commercials these days are the most expensive form of advertising and are considered so potent and effective in convincing people how to think, act and consume that enormous sums of money are paid for 60-second placement ads during massive viewing events like the Super Bowl. Marketing and psychological studies have obviously proven their effectiveness, otherwise companies would not be paying the huge sums of money they do to be guaranteed a "spot" for an ad placement.

Advertisements can change our way of thinking about products, but can potentially change the way we think about and view ourselves as well. Think of the number of times a day we see women depicted in advertisements, print or screen, as being large-breasted, having perfect skin, well-toned bodies, luscious, shiny (and mostly long) hair – many times a day! Not uncommonly, such women are often portrayed as helpless, rarely powerful and seldom in a position of power or authority over males. Movies, television, video and video gaming offer the same portrayals in their formats as well. We may find it humorous or cute to see women portrayed this way, but the impact is anything but funny for women. From bitch to babe to sex object to maid and mother, every single repeated image continually reinforces our thinking (men's and women's both) that women are not to be taken seriously.

Have you ever stopped to consider who largely owns and controls the media? Or the executives are who in the end have authority over what gets produced, published and promoted? Although most media producers will tell you that they are simply meeting the needs and wants of their audience, they are definitely not meeting the needs of what women want in the media. It's largely a one-sided gender bias as to what kinds of programs and what kinds of stereo-types get flashed across our TV and computer screens as well as the media we are subjected to in everyday ads outside the home.

In the 1980s, Noam Chomsky became famous with the documentary, *Manufacturing Consent*, which described how the media is owned and manipulated by a handful of people in mega-media corporations. He taught us all to be suspect of media and continually question both its source and its motives. Another recent documentary highlighting this problem is *Miss Representation*, discussed below.

The Bottom Line. Television, movies, advertisements, radio, the Internet and all other media play a major role in impacting our behavior. This media is the main way that socially-desired expectations are passed on to the masses. For women, however, not only are many media messages harmful, the producers of the media are primarily men. This, of course, explains why so many TV sitcoms, TV dramas and movies almost completely ignore women, degrade women and generally promote gender stereotypes. The media impact is extraordinarily powerful and stereotyping is extraordinarily harmful and not a joking matter.

What To Do. We must educate ourselves to be much more aware of sexism in the media and we must consider who controls the media and look to change this by way of equal representation. We must refuse to tolerate any media that casts women in outdated stereotypical roles.

We need to watch documentaries by organizations such as the Media Education Corporation that describe the insidiousness of the media. Every parent and teen should take a "media awareness" course, stop watching sexist media and challenge those who produce sexist programs to take more responsibility for the harm they cause. We must insist that change happen now. If, for example, we refuse to be the audience by turning off our TVs, bypassing movie theaters and refusing to purchase magazines, the media will get the message.

Chapter 7

Don't Expect Women to Be Beauty Models

"I regard the premeditated and calculated attempt by advertisers to promote products by lowering female self-esteem as despicable and misogynistic. Creating the illusion in both sexes that an acceptable woman is a statuesque, ultra beautiful, emaciated, long-legged waif is diabolical." ~ Nicky Marone

The next time you're in the checkout line at your local grocery store, look at the magazine covers on display at eye level as you wait. On any given shopping trip, I can usually count about 20 cover photos of women staring out at me from the magazine racks. These images of women are not like you and me. The faces and bodies portrayed are flawless: beautiful skin, perky breasts, slim thighs and waists, smooth, silky hair, perfect teeth that produce a spectacular smile.

These are our female role models. They are not real, yet they are the beauty standard that has been, and continues to be, created by our society. Their images not only define the precise eyes, nose, eyebrows, skin and hair that you and I need, they also send a clear message about the value of women in our society. In one simple stop at the grocery and/or drugstore we are reminded not only that we must be stunningly beautiful, but that beauty is a woman's most important characteristic, her most essential power above all else.

At its core, a women's beauty is defined in relation to men. In other words, for a woman to be beautiful, she must be attractive to men. She must have perfect facial features and a slim body. She must have vibrant hair and skin, hair-free under arms and legs and she must smell delightful and be smiling at all times. To be valued she must present her public self in a way that is appealing to men, no matter how uncomfortable this might be. This includes plucking eyebrows, shaving legs, dying hair, applying make-up, wearing high heels and squeezing into tight girdles or spandex under-attire or other devices manufactured to hide true body figures in order to achieve a desirable shape.

The unfortunate presumption in all of this is that women want to please men and, of course, want to take part in this outward physical presentation because the goal of every woman is to attract a man, possibly to marry or gain power and status through him. Sadly, it's not just advertisers convincing women to consume clothing, make-up, hair products and a multitude of self-improvement practices to improve their appearance, but rather a whole society telling us that if we, as women, want to be happy we must be appealing to men and therein be the envy of other women.

Author, Selma Greenberg describes it this way:

> The demand that girls be pretty and women be beautiful is perhaps the most persistent and oppressive of all demands made on women. While it is clear that meeting the cultural beauty standard is better than not meeting it, why is it an issue of such high priority? Perhaps because it's so convenient for males and so inconvenient for females. Beautiful females become just another reward for high status men. Beauty is highly visible and fits amazingly well with the notion of woman as possession or adjunct to man.

The cost of this constant beauty pressure is not just a cost on women's self-esteem, but also a literal cost to women's pocketbooks. In order to maintain this standard of beauty and to feel good about ourselves we are told that we need to continually buy, shop and consume.

From a very young age, the message is very specific: We must buy makeup, clothes and other things to make ourselves better than what we are. In other words, there is something inherently "wrong" with us and we need to correct that wrong by consuming more things – from face cream to diet pills to high heel shoes. Yet, advertisers and manufacturers of the multitude of things that we "need" are not implicitly evil. They are often just another tool of our culture – the transmitter of our society's ideas about women. We tell them as a society that it's okay that women spend billions of dollars every year on useless products. We think that women buying and consuming more things is good.

In order to meet these high standards, women are required to improve themselves significantly, usually by purchasing manufacturers' products. It's not sufficient to have clean hair; our hair must also be silky, thick, smooth, fluffy, shiny, tousled, wavy and radiant. Our skin must be soft, supple, shiny, smooth, luminous, radiant, lean and firm. The amount of time and money we are successfully persuaded to spend on products is mind-boggling!

What makes this pressure to be beautiful so ultimately damning, however, is the suggestion that without beauty, women have little to offer society. Indeed, we are sold the idea that beauty is the ultimate power for women – not our brains, our physical strength or our contributions to the world. It's not enough to gain professional status in a variety of fields. Women physicians, lawyers, judges and even those holding executive or political office – such as Hillary Clinton with her resume of accomplishments – are still expected to be stunning and elegant.

To make matters even worse, because this imposed notion of beauty is so aggressively narrow, only a handful of young women under the age of 25 can actually attain it fully. The rest of us are forever on an endless treadmill trying to realize a level of beauty that is frankly unachievable, given the reality of aging and the fact that women have a multitude of body types to begin with. Not only that, even if we were to come close to reaching the standard, it would cost a fortune in plastic surgery to maintain it as we age. Sadly, many women who strive to maintain their beauty well into their 30s, 40s and 50s ultimately face rejection from society and their husbands/partners if or when they decide they no longer want to seek to beautify themselves simply to be valued.

Beauty messaging essentially tells women that they are inadequate. Here are some of the subtle, yet demeaning, messages women hear on a daily basis.

- You are born imperfect, plain; you are not attractive.

- You must change something about yourself to be acceptable; to be valued.

- You need to adhere to current fashion trends to look appealing.

- You must wear makeup to cover your facial imperfections.

- You must wear accessories and ornaments to decorate yourself and make yourself appealing to men.

- Watch your weight; be careful of what you eat. Being slim will increase your value.

- It's unattractive to look muscular, strong or naturally healthy.

One of the most debilitating consequences of this beauty pressure is the resulting self-hatred that many women feel, particularly toward their bodies. Many are reluctant to show their body shapes; others can be hesitant or fearful of their body shape in case it brings them unwanted attention. Not surprisingly, many women struggle to love their own body in a world where the female body is put on display and measured for worth by outsiders. In this societal environment, where body parts reflect female value, how do we help girls to accept and value their bodies? Their breasts? Their legs? Their buttocks? Their own sexuality?

The media's failure to achieve constructive and meaningful messaging to and for women was brought home to me in a recent screening of a documentary entitled, *Miss Representation*. This well-documented film addresses the impact of the beauty pressure and its consequences for young women and discusses how repeated messaging of females as beauty objects inevitably leads to a valuation of women based solely on their looks. The film informs the viewer that both men and women interpret the endless messaging as fact: women's value is in their appearance and little else.

Miss Representation reveals how little power women truly have in society, how they are barely represented in the media and other institutions (other than to acknowledge their looks) and how, as a result, they remain out of decision-making positions that shape our society, thereby rendering women even less powerful and effective. As Jean Kilbourne says in the film, "Girls get the message, from very early on, that what's most important is how they look; that their value, their worth, depends on that. And boys get the message that this is what's important about girls.... No matter what else a woman does, no matter what else her achievements, their value *still* depends on how they look."

The Bottom Line. Societal pressure on women to be beautiful and sexual is staggering! Evidence of this appears daily in media everywhere, from magazines to TV, movies and videogames where women's faces and bodies are on display in sexualized poses. These images are part of a larger society-wide message that tells women that they must attain the standard of beauty that has been set by men, and that they must use any and all means possible, from make-up to surgery, to achieve this standard of beauty that realistically is only achievable for a small percentage of very young women. The carrot that dangles is that this beauty is power; this beauty is success; this beauty is self-worth above all. The fall-out for women has been, and continues to be, the erosion of self-esteem.

What To Do. Collectively, we must stop and take a very close look at why we as a society place so much pressure on women to be attractive and sexually appealing to men. We must challenge the entire notion that a woman's beauty is her primary source of power and worth and instead start honoring women for "all" of who they are.

We must admit that this very costly focus on beauty is not only absurd, but that it holds back women from engaging fully and equally in constructive and productive pursuits and goals. In the short term, we must reject all media that promotes and perpetuates beauty as the defining aspect of a women's worth in society. We must celebrate women in all shapes and sizes; in all manner of looks and attire. We must reject products from companies that use advertising that equates women's worth with beauty. I encourage women to speak with their wallets, in both how you buy beauty products and examine why you buy beauty products.

The best way to prevent the negative impact of media pressure is awareness. Learn how to critique the media and develop media-sensitive savvy. Question what you read and what you accept as truth about women. Read and view alternative media. The Internet is a great source for that.

Here are some other suggestions that you may find helpful in getting off of the beauty treadmill.

- Avoid cosmetic and perfume departments.

- Watch movies that have positive depictions of women.

- Carefully screen videos and video games, particularly for children.

- Don't buy products that advertise in a way that degrades women.

- Cut out sexist ads and mail them back to magazines with a note of displeasure.

- Write to companies whose advertisements are offensive.

Part Two

Loss of the Feminine

Chapter 8

Eradicate Pornography and the Sexualization of Women and Girls

"Increasingly women have been sexualized and objectified, their bodies marketed to sell tractors and toothpaste. Soft- and hard-core pornography is everywhere. Sexual and physical assaults on girls are at an all-time high." ~ Mary Pipher

I recently travelled to Las Vegas and realized that although the city is touted as an "adult Disneyland," unlike Disneyland, women aren't necessarily having "fun." It's all in the perception and obviously depends on who's judging this "fun"-land. Most of the activities (like topless female servers in bars) are designed by men and for men's pleasure. Women visitors may not only find it difficult to find their idea of fun, but because so much of the so-called fun involves the sexualization of women, engaging in the fun can be downright awkward and distasteful. Indeed, given the abundance of male drunkenness and excessive leering ("what happens in Vegas stays in Vegas" expresses all you might imagine), Las Vegas can be a downright scary place for many women, both for those who work there and for those who visit.

In my opinion, this is not an adult playground; it's a man's playground. From what I saw, most of the men are very comfortably dressed in jeans and runners (e.g., un-sexy) while a good percentage of the women are dressed very upscale (not to mention, very sexually). My daughters joked that we should design a Las Vegas for women with calming music and yoga studios. We agreed that our designs would not include the objectification and sexualizing of men as something "fun" to do.

One of the best eye-openers on our societal sexualizing of girls and women is a documentary called *Killing Us Softly*. Based on her powerful lecture, Jean Kilbourne describes the way in which magazines, television, advertising and video games sexualize and demean women and girls. Her collection of media images and her brilliant commentary is powerful and disturbing. And although she mostly blames the media and suggests solutions like avoiding sexist magazines (e.g., as much as 90% of all magazines) and refusing to buy products that sexualize females (e.g., 82% of all products), the real problem is an entire culture that accepts sexualizing girls and women as not only okay, but expected.

Sadly, Kilbourne notes that in over 30 years of observing societal trends and the treatment of women, she cannot point to any significant improvements in the media images of girls or women. On the contrary, in many cases advertisements have become more demeaning and sexualized in recent years. The message is the same in each decade's advertising depiction of women: we are objectified in a sexualized manner by ads that reflect and encourage a patriarchal and sexist vision. Such societal messages are impacting women's spirit and stifling our abilities from a very young age to shine and thrive. Through repeated negative media messaging we are continually harming women's self-esteem and preventing them from seeing and achieving their full potential.

I used to get angry at my husband when he said I looked beautiful. He could never understand what "my" problem was. At first I thought that I was just overly shy or that my low self-esteem prevented me from accepting a compliment (which is very common in women of my generation). For years I felt that his glances at me were more lustful than loving. His choice of words, like, "you are so sexy" just made me cringe. For many years I often felt ashamed by his "compliments" until I began to understand what was really happening. It had to do with the word "sexy."

Early in my research on women in society, I realized that the definition of the word "sexy" was derived from a male perspective.

Indeed, the word has been contrived and manipulated so that it is no longer significant or meaningful to women. When we think "sexy," we inevitably think "sexy to a man" or "tantalizing to a man." We've been subconsciously trained, through endless media imaging, to act "sexy" towards a man in a way that will make him happy.

The word "sexy" rarely means the things that might make a woman feel aroused or sexy, like closeness and intimacy. Indeed, because of this, women often feel inordinate pressure in relationships to "perform" in a sexual manner and, as they mature, struggle with their sexuality because they never learned what really makes them "feel" sexy. We've been taught how to be sexually useful and appealing to men.

An example of this can be found again in our simple marketing messages. Car ads suggest to men that they have a chance to have sex with a woman like the one displayed on top of the car in the advertisement if they buy that kind of vehicle. Shaving cream ads suggest they'll wake up in bed in the morning with a woman like the one in the commercial if they choose the right shaving cream.

Although we somehow accept the fact that "sex sells" we do not look at what is really going on. What is being sold and subsequently bought? Girls' and women's sexuality. What does that sexuality look like? More often than not, big pouty lips, large breasts and, not uncommonly, shapely, open legs. The woman's sexuality is an enticement for men. She is used as a pawn in the advertising world and her purpose is to stimulate a man to take action. The goal is simply to make men think (subconsciously) that they will receive sex (or power through sex) by buying the particular product. Buried in this sexual selling are very clear messages that women and girls and men and boys all see and hear.

- Females can be used as objects to sell things.

- Men want sex all the time and will purchase things it they think they will get sex.

- Only women who are beautiful and slim are sexually attractive to men.

- Women who are not beautiful are irrelevant and don't have a purpose to men.

It's not just men who get sucked into the "sex sells" messages. Women fall as well and sadly suffer because of it. The darkest side of the sexualization of girls and women are the pornography and sex-trade industries. Indeed, the recent popularity of the book, *Shades of Grey* (which is essentially about a woman who is psychologically controlled and tortured), just shows how our society not only accepts pornography as normal, but even sensationalizes it. Not surprisingly, the popularity of this book has been linked to increased incidences of violence to women.

Pornography websites are often owned by misogynists (women haters) who believe that buying and selling women to men is fine. Though a most debased form of "entertainment" for men, pornography reflects our society-held view that women are second-class citizens whose value is purely and simply relative to men. It's mind-boggling that a civilized society would allow this notion and treatment of women as sex-slaves to happen, but it does. By casting pornography, and most particularly pornography that depicts physical harm and degradation to women, as being a "freedom of choice," we as a society deny the huge cost to women as a whole.

Other insidious industries that make money from degrading girls and women or that aim to "put women in their place" include the video gaming and music industries. Both are notorious for sexualizing and demeaning women. Kilbourne's documentary provides one such video game advertisement that shows a beautiful woman's body being dumped in the trunk of a car with a well-dressed man standing nearby!

In her book, *Reflections of the Moon on Water,* Xiaolan Zhao suggests that by simply looking at magazines and videos we all might get the sense that women's *raison d'être* is to fulfill a man's wants and desires.

> It seems women are conditioned to accept stereotypes of women and men that reinforce notions of what we must look like and do to keep men happy. When the emphasis in sex is on the men's desires and satisfaction, there is less room for the fulfillment of our own needs. Women fake orgasms because we want to please our partners. We are concerned that our partners may feel inadequate if we don't climax, since we've been told that so much of men's self-esteem is connected to their sexual prowess, and to threaten our partner's self-esteem may endanger the very foundation of our relationship.

Author Ken Dolan-Del Vecchio explains that pornography is not just harmful to women, but also to male/female relationships. As he says, most boys experience their first sexual encounters with pornographic magazines, videos and online images rather than with a real physically-present human being. These images are air-brushed to perfection and the models are never tired and always ready for sex.

Boys come to believe not only that this is what sex "looks" like, but also what the ideal female partner looks and acts like. Even worse, boys and men are led to believe that they are entitled to receive sex from those they find sexually appealing and that the main purpose of sex is a man's sexual gratification. After all, women, in the pornographic picture are irrelevant and disposable after orgasm. As Dolan-Del Vecchio says, "The idea of a mutually respectful, loving and gratifying relationship with another human being as the optimum context for sex mystifies many men. In fact ... we often find this kind of closeness as a sexual turn-off. We see this type of connection as boring, stodgy, and drained of excitement."

Marianne Williamson explains the difference between erotica and pornography in this way, "Erotica celebrates women and sexuality. Pornography violates women and demeans sex. Since most pornography is the psychic rape of women, not men, then it must be women who collectively turn the tide back."

The Bottom Line. Women today are subjected to intense and endless sexualization that we as a society blindly accept as if it were natural and normal. This sexualization not only degrades those women being sexualized, but all women. It also impacts our sense of self-esteem and subconsciously suggests to us all that we are second-class citizens and are not worthy of better treatment. We tolerate the selling of girls' and women's sexuality as if it were men's right or an equal commercial exchange, failing to admit that females sell their bodies when they lack money, often in desperation, and by buying sex, men abuse their power and often contribute to the cycle of violence and control over women. Our society accepts that it is okay to make women into sex objects in a variety of ways. We permit the use of women's bodies as selling tools for everything from cars to jack hammers. We allow pornography and women-hating to run rampant and unchecked. This is not normal; it demeans women and reduces women's self-worth.

What To Do. We need to admit that sexualizing girls and women harms both women and our society. We must reject this sexualization and forms of media and products that carry this message. We have to question why we tolerate and even promote violence against women, particularly in video games and films. We need to stop pretending that pornographic violence is eroticism and notice the misogyny behind it. We must pay close attention to the harm of pornography to young boys and to their healthy sexual relationships. We must attack and eradicate the ever-growing sex trade of girls and young women by not just prosecuting abusers but by making any abuse of women completely unacceptable.

Chapter 9

Challenge the Tyranny of Niceness

"Are you a victim of what talk show host Oprah Winfrey calls the disease to please? Do you constantly worry about what others will think? If you do, you are not alone. Most women want to be liked – to be popular. Locked in the sophomoric mentality of high school, we all secretly want to be a popular cheerleader, or the prom queen. However, this insatiable quest to be miss congeniality creates problems for us professionally." ~ Susan Solovic

As a society, we not only expect women to be beautiful and sexy, we also expect them to be beneficial, useful and terribly "nice." We expect women to be helpful, kind, generous and always support-ive of others – and to be happy. This means that women must do things that will generally make the lives of everyone around them more comfortable. In my book *Wake up Sleeping Beauty!*, I describe this pressure: "Girls, unlike boys, are told that they must nice no matter what. It's not an option. This causes many problems but pri-marily a loss of self. By being overly nice girls sacrifice a part of who they are and lose touch with their healthy boundaries that enable them to know the depths of who they are and their own needs, not just the needs of others. They lose the ability to say 'no' without feeling bad."

As young women we learn that in order to be successful we must be hyper-aware and attentive to the feelings of others and to also take care of others. As teens, we learn that our friendships and being popular are critical to our survival. We learn that we must be nice to absolutely everyone and that to have no friends or to be disliked is suicidal. In my book *Lean Out,* I describe this pressure:

> Perhaps the most harmful socialization involves the pressure to be nice. Often called the "tyranny of niceness," girls and women are required to be nice to absolutely everyone. As described by Babcock and Laschever: "Despite all the gains we've made, one double standard (at least) persists: In our society we expect women to be nice. And it's not just that we like nice women. We think women *should* be nice – warm, pleasant, friendly. When women behave in ways that we don't perceive as warm, pleasant, and friendly...we react negatively."

This pressure to be nice is regularly reinforced and perpetuated in the media. As demonstrated in the documentary, *Killing Us Softly*, author Jean Kilbourne comments: "In parents' magazines, boys are active and girls are passive. A boy plays on the jungle gym in one ad, while in another a girl stands quietly looking down and holding some flowers. Girls are often shown as playful clowns, perpetuating the attitude that girls and women are childish and cannot be taken seriously, whereas even the very young men are generally portrayed as secure, powerful and serious." The message to be silent, small, and easy to manipulate shows up often in advertisements that effectively "cut women down to size." As Kilbourne says, "In ad after ad, girls are urged to be 'barely there' – beautiful, but silent. Many ads in teen magazines feature girls and young women in very passive poses, limp, doll-like, sometimes acting like little girls...."

A recent book by Sharon Lamb and Lyn Mikel Brown entitled, *Packaging Girlhood,* describes the many "stereotypical, demeaning, limiting and alarming" images of girls that are regularly being packaged and sold to our daughters. It's an eye-opening read and one worth seeking out, especially valuable for those with daughters who want to understand the insidious nature of marketing campaigns directed at young girls and how to combat their effects.

As young women, we learn how to automatically smile, even when we don't feel like it. Not uncommonly, many women feel a sense of guilt when they say anything negative against someone. Of course, there are those who do not, but if we speak generally, a very large percentage of women aren't comfortable with *not* being nice. Females are not inherently born with this trait or a desire to become nicer-than-nice martyrs. We've been taught to be this way and the expectation of "nice" is reinforced every day by almost every single person we come in contact with.

When it comes to relating to men, these expectations of niceness escalate. Women learn early on that they are not to compete directly with men or appear threatening to men. This usually means being agreeable and even silent or passive. It means never placing oneself above a male, intellectually, socially or in stature. Some of the hidden messages conveyed to girls and women through advertising in television and magazines today look like this:

- Respect and idolize the man in your life, no matter how he treats you.

- Support "your man" in his pursuits (yours are secondary).

- Maintain the comforts of home and expect no pay or acknowledgement.

- Plan, prepare and make your husband's and your family's meals.

- Care for your children is solely your job.

- Arrange and attend to you and your husband's social life.

- Look good so that other men will envy your husband.

- Be a super-woman and do not complain.

I recall a joke I heard as a college student that goes like this:

Question: What's a perfect woman look like?
Answer: She's 3 feet high, with a flat head to hold my beer and
              pizza while I watch TV.

Men find this joke quite funny even though it's obviously degrading and demeaning to women. Our society has encouraged men to believe that laughing about women is not only acceptable, but expected.

Taught to be non-threatening, women hide their brilliance and downplay their accomplishments and strengths often trying to be smaller than they are. Women learn to never show public distain for any man, for fear of "provoking" an attack or being labelled a man-hater. Women must never embarrass or undermine men. So the equation looks like this: Be appealing, beautiful, sexy, adore males and never appear threatening to them.

This endless pressure to be nice and not rock the status quo has a very obvious impact: It causes women to work like crazy trying to satisfy men and it causes other problems related to self-sacrifice like exhaustion, resentment and self-hatred. We label the problem the "disease to please" or the "tyranny of niceness" as if it is some temporary illness that can be easily cured – by women, of course.

And to make matters worse, after raising girls to be nicer than nice, we turn around and blame and criticize them when, as women, they end up sacrificing too much of themselves for others and suffer emotionally as a result. And because it's their "fault," we tell them that they need to stop it somehow, even though this later message is in direct opposition to the continual daily messaging of "put others first."

This double-message conundrum means women don't just go crazy from the burden of being constantly nice and giving too much of themselves, they also go crazy from the criticism laid against them of being "too nice." It's a complex line to navigate and since it's a "women's problem," we women get no help whatsoever from the real source of the problem: a whole society that benefits from nice women.

The following is a great example from a business book by Susan Solovic of the double messaging directed at women:

> To be a dynamic leader, you have to face the facts – not everyone is going to like you. There are some people who aren't going to like you because you remind them of their mother-in-law or their former wife. Others may dislike you because they are envious of your talents and success. But success in business is not based on popularity. Successful women recognize the difference between business and friendship. They can make a tough call, and when someone takes exception, they can deal with it without falling part.

The excerpt above suggests that most women are oversensitive, care too much about what others think and that this is a weakness. It tells us that this behavior is not only distasteful, but that it is causing women to be unsuccessful. The paragraph also suggests that mothers-in-law, ex-wives and women that have a degree of success are targets of derision and contempt by men and that it's completely reasonable for men in the workplace to judge you based on those other women they may know.

Sadly, this excerpt, by its very warning to women that they may risk not being liked plays into the belief that women are weak and thin-skinned and therefore not suited to a business environment. It fails to acknowledge and appreciate the fact that women's desire to be liked is not only a positive attribute, but is instilled in females from childhood. It also undermines the value that women bring to the workplace by being and acting as "the mortar between the bricks," or the warm human touch in an often cold work environment.

The pressure to be nice comes at a high cost to women. Many women end up compromising their own goals and sacrificing their own needs so that people around them – their husband/boyfriend, family, coworkers – are able to achieve their goals and objectives. In the process, women retreat and convince themselves that their own needs don't matter or they become bitter over the sacrifices they've had to make along the way.

The Bottom Line. As a society we place enormous pressure on women to be helpful and terribly nice. We expect them to be kind, generous and supportive in ways not expected of men. This drives women to become victim to the so-called "tyranny of niceness" where they sacrifice themselves for others. Then we, as a society, criticize them for doing this and expect them to somehow change or not let the fallout of this unending niceness affect their demeanor.

As a society we fail to take the blame because all of us, though particularly men, benefit when half the population is not only nice, but kind, helpful, agreeable and self-sacrificing. This urging of females to sacrifice themselves is abuse in a very subtle form and to allow or encourage women to shrink and downplay their brilliance is nothing short of a travesty.

What To Do. We must stop expecting women to be so nice. We must notice the ways in which we pressure women to be agreeable, silent and passive. We must take a very close look at why we as a society place so much pressure on women to behave agreeably. We must admit that this "tyranny" is costly to women and holds them back.

We must support women in being honest and authentic and in choosing their own course and endeavors and not expect them to be selfless. We must allow them to be whoever they really are: sad, happy, angry, irritable, enthusiastic, intelligent, aggressive, etc. Whatever it is, we must never expect females to be "happy slaves" and must acknowledge the harm caused by this simple expectation. We must celebrate strong women, without the need to compare them to men.

Chapter 10

Value the Intelligence of Emotions

"Females traditionally have the power to intuit, to surrender and to feel. This power is about people and relationships and healing the heart and nurturing the spirit. It is a power that communicates and shares. A power that rests on the belief that all people are powerful and all people deserve to be treated equally." ~ Anita Roberts

I sometimes watch the evening news on television. It always surprises me that the announcers are so calm and composed when reporting on devastating worldwide tragedies and horrific deaths. I am surprised in some measure that the news doesn't bring them to tears. How are they able to contain their emotions when reading about such horrible human sadness and despair? We all learn how to contain our emotions, I know, but when we do it too much, we risk becoming like robots – insensitive and incapable of responding and treating others with empathy and concern.

Most of us, though particularly men, have learned that it is not appropriate to show emotions in public and most particularly inappropriate to show emotions in the workplace. Even extreme laughter and joy are considered inappropriate and frowned upon. Messages such as "check your emotions at the door" and "the workplace is no place for tears" come through loud and clear. It's as if there's an underlying concern that if a person expresses strong emotions that we may all collapse into blubbering messes; as though chaos will result and professionalism will disappear. Especially in the workplace, the underlying message is such that if we allow any emotions then everyone will spend all of their time emoting and never get anything done. This thinking seems quite narrow, not to mention condescending to women, as it's women that society really fears will emote. Apparently we can't be trusted enough to be able to manage our own emotions and decide what is appropriate and inappropriate.

The stifling of emotions takes a particular toll on women. We are shamed for crying, raising our voice or expressing any emotion in a manner that is not fitting with how men emote. We are told repeatedly from a young age that we are "too sensitive" (even though "sensitive" is what society has trained us to be) and that we should grow "thicker skin." We are accused of taking things too personally and of getting "worked up" at the "the smallest thing." We're told to "take a pill." Imagine that, being told to pacify ourselves by taking drugs. Unfortunately, this was a common mantra in the 50s, 60s and 70s; doctors readily prescribed drugs for women because they were "emotional."

When women are discouraged from expressing emotions they often feel, in effect, that they are being asked to sever a critical part of who they are. They are forced to discard a part of their natural skill set. Inevitably, they eventually feel shut down. They are told that if they are too emotive they risk compromising their effectiveness, efficiency and even their chance for success. Indeed, in some work environments, even attributes like collaboration and relationship building (traits that women are well versed in) are frowned upon because they are considered "unprofessional." Any such workplaces should think twice about this attitude.

When we tell women to stop showing emotions we are in effect telling them not to respond in a way that feels normal and natural to them and that their instinctive response is inappropriate. This causes women to not trust their feelings, which often leads to uncertainty and insecurity.

It seems odd to me that we continue to tell women to be less emotional when there is extensive research on both emotional and social Intelligence (mostly conducted by men) showing that emotions, empathy, creativity and intuition are not only extraordinarily powerful, but quite necessary to our ability to think and make decisions.

Here, from Solovic, is a typical example of how a professional woman uses her emotional intelligence (in this case, through compliments, which is essentially a direct response and acknowledgement of others). Rather than celebrating this ability, society often dismisses and condemns the skill as personal "chit chat" and not as important as the "nitty gritty" stuff:

> Right in the middle of a meeting about a company's strategic plan, one woman might stop and comment on how much she likes the other woman's earrings. They'll spend a few minutes discussing jewelry, and then it will be right back to the nitty-gritty of the business issues without ever missing a beat. Women can do this because they easily shift between right-brain and left-brain activities. On the other hand, men are linear thinkers, and they aren't comfortable bouncing back and forth. Most men would find that kind of conversation disruptive, and they would be frustrated by the lack of focus. Unless a man interjects personal chit chat, stick to the business issues at hand.

Research is emerging that shows females are more empathetic than males and may be born with an innate capacity to sense the feelings of others. As Eve Ensler, creator of The Vagina Monologues, says in her powerful off-Broadway show, "We are emotional beings!" The point is that we cannot and should not turn that part of our being "off."

According to Anita Roberts, author of *Safe Teens*, females, more so than males, are wired by hormones and brain patterns to:

- Read body language and emotion,

- Speak and read at an early age,

- Live longer lives,

- Be less likely to get major diseases,

- Have wider peripheral vision, and

- Have stronger links between the two sides of the brain.

Slowly we are all learning about the importance of emotional intelligence and the fact that passion can drive excellence. Without it, commitment and motivation can be lacking and work can become boring and meaningless.

Social intelligence too is coming to the forefront as an indispensable life skill. The ability to work well with others and build relationships is critical to work, yet we fail to notice that women are masters of relationships. Women are the glue that holds the pieces of our communities, workplaces and society together. Yet, they are often accused of being too chatty or social simply because they are different than men.

The following is a list of some of the very necessary day-to-day tasks that require significant social and emotional intelligence that women's skill set so readily offers:

- Conflict resolution

- Writing letters and expressing opinions clearly

- Mediation

- A sense of caring and relating to

- The ability to empathize

- The ability to lead and take charge

- Public speaking

- Fundraising

- Community building

- Collaboration

- Networking

- Assessing situations and people

Related to emotional intelligence is an often condemned ability called "intuition." Intuition is an internal "knowing" that often shows itself as a strong physical sensation, like a tingling feeling. It has rarely to do with facts and evidence so much as it has to do with a hunch or premonition. There is some suggestion that it's our human way of tapping an invisible energy source. Unfortunately, in Western culture, because this cannot be verified, it very often gets dismissed as flakey or unfounded, particularly as it is a skill often held more by women than men. For girls and women, their intuition is often their best friend and should be both valued and encouraged.

The Bottom Line. We continually accuse women of being too emotional and tell them their emotions are "problematic." Women are told not to cry, not to raise their voice, not to swear, not to get "too excited." This expectation and pressure causes many women to reject integral parts of themselves and implies that this aspect of their being is inappropriate and therefore not valued. Holding in emotions is not only problematic for women, but research increasingly shows that emotions are a valuable part of critical thinking and should be acknowledged and embraced.

What To Do. As women, we must stop rejecting aspects of our emotions and embrace them fully as normal ways of expressing ourselves and important sources of information. We must learn to trust our instincts and intuition fully. As a society, we must stop telling women that emotions are bad or inappropriate. We must help men and women accept and better understand the value of emotions and how to view them in a constructive and positive way. When someone suggests that a woman is being overly emotional, ask them this: What do you think the appropriate response should be and why?

Chapter 11

Remember Women's History

"They overcame great obstacles, suffered setbacks, knew hardship, and endured public scorn and ridicule. But they were not deterred from their belief in themselves and their mission." ~ Nicky Marone

One of the most impactful books I have ever read is called, *Who Cooked the Last Supper* written by Professor Rosalind Miles. Originally titled, *Women's History of the World*, this book describes in plain language, the entire history of women, from the beginning of time to today. Although it is an amazing book in that it pulls together the bulk of women's history, Dr. Miles explains why the book is so short and the difficulties she had in locating information about women's lives. In a nutshell, for thousands of years women were not allowed to participate in any sort of public life and were restricted in speaking and writing. As a result, almost nothing was written "by women" or "about women." Our history is essentially just that – a version of "his-story" and not her-story.

The entire concept of "the feminine" disappeared over 3,000 years ago. Before then, there were many goddess cultures and societies around the world that honored the earth and its cycles, attributing great value to women and feminine traits. Many thousands of years ago, men and women lived together as equals. Indeed, women were worshipped for their ability to give life through their bodies. Both men and women were respected as fully contributing and indispensable members in the societies in which they lived. Over time, these cultures slowly disappeared and were replaced with dominance-based cultures or patriarchies.

Author and lecturer, Marianne Williamson, describes it in this way:

> Archaeological evidence now argues for the existence of a twenty-thousand year period of history when men and women lived as equals, with neither sex dominating the other. The earth flourished. The so-called feminine qualities of compassion, nurturing and non-violence were shared by men and women alike and were the most vital elements of social structure. Women were revered as priest-esses and healers. Our intuitive strengths were not scorned, but respected.

One of the best books ever written about the fall of women is the bestseller, *The Chalice and the Blade*, by Riane Eisler. It describes a prehistoric age when women were revered as keepers of life and knowledge. In these goddess-centered societies respect for the land prevailed and women were honored and revered, rather than dominated and despised.

Eisler describes the work of early anthropologists who discovered many ancient female-based and goddess cultures and how these civilizations were destroyed and re-claimed under the guise of modern religion. Evidence of this downfall is reflected in religious images that evolved to reflect a societal shift towards fear and war. Eisler refers to the image of Jesus bleeding on the cross and asks, "If the central religious image was of a woman giving birth and not, as in our time, a man dying on a cross, it would not be unreasonable to infer that life and the love of life – rather than death and the fear of death – were dominant in society as well as art."

History shows that our more immediate ancestors built societies that placed men firmly at the top of a hierarchy of living things. Women's areas of knowledge, which were the earth-based practices and life-based rituals, were eventually labelled as witchcraft and paganism and women were not only scorned, but often accused and punished severely for heresy. Male-based churches took power and placed women under the control of husbands and fathers. It is estimated that about 100,000 witches or female healers and intellectuals were burned at the stake during this time of transition that saw women's role change from equality, power and respect to subservience.

When the goddess societies fell, so too did the honoring of women, girls and all that is feminine. What also fell was the great skill and potential contribution of half of the population; the feminine way of being and hundreds of feminine rituals, practices and celebrations were devalued and discarded. The elevation of males combined with the devaluing of females resulted in the degradation and sexualization of women and the condemnation of feminine characteristics that persist to this day.

This historical regression explains why, for thousands of years, women were denied access to the same basic rights and freedoms offered to men. Women were, and still are in some cultures around the world (and even in some of our own western religious rituals), considered the possessions of their fathers or husbands (a father "gives" his daughter in marriage to the groom is a leftover example in western culture). Any activities that women engaged in had to be approved of by males; unfortunately, some cultures still practice this today. All family fortunes were passed along to the male heir and, consequently, if a woman did not marry, she was often destitute.

The women's suffrage movement changed much of the state of affairs for women. Suffragettes fought for women's rights as "people" and for equal access to the vote and to paid jobs. The movement began in the United States in the mid-1800s. Two of the originators of the movement were Susan B. Anthony and Elizabeth Stanton. Anthony was a young teacher of Quaker descent. Her Quaker heritage instilled a sense of social equity and from an early age she was an anti-slavery activist and believed in equity for blacks as well as equity for women. She believed in and asked for equal pay in her position as a teacher. Stanton had a keen interest in law and justice from an early age and together with her husband was an anti-slavery activist as well.

Both women were pivotal in the suffrage movement. Anthony managed to vote in an election in Rochester, New York, in 1872. Though she was subsequently arrested and charged for doing so, her actions and unrelenting persistence alongside those of other women led the way for American women to be granted the right to vote. The long and hard battle succeeded on August 26, 1920. At that time, women were 51% of the US population.

Fortunately, the work of abolitionists, as well as the work of prohibitionists and early labor activists, helped in the fight to improve justice and equality in the United States. Such groups were instrumental in seeing to the introduction of many laws that made children and women's lives less difficult; child labor laws, birth control and the improvement of working conditions in sweat shops can be attributed to them, as well as ending the ridiculous practice of women wearing tight corsets that often broke their ribs and prevented them from breathing properly.

In the 1960s, consciousness-raising groups in North America questioned many societal assumptions that held women back, such as why all women were considered and expected to be housekeepers. They drew attention to the hidden culture of male entitlement and questioned the societal systems that benefited some (mostly white men) and harmed others (mostly women and non-whites generally). The main focus of that revolution was to eliminate unfair discrimination against all kinds of groups such as African Americans, visible minorities and women.

The feminist movement, which has gone through many ups and downs over the last hundred-plus years, continues to challenge inequality at many levels. From everyday sexism to systemic barriers, it is rightly credited for many of women's advancements. Women now not only have the right to vote, but we also have the right to attend university, the right to own property and the right to work for pay. Feminists continue to fight for equal pay, access to abortions, flexible work hours and social justice and security.

The Bottom Line. As a society we have forgotten women's history. We have forgotten that women have only recently been recognized as citizens and given rights to vote and participate in public life. Until very recently women were not allowed to vote, to own property, to go to university or to work for pay. Women were not allowed to serve as church ministers, hold elected offices or run businesses. To this day, women are not allowed to be priests in the Catholic Church (let alone to even think of becoming the Pope). A hundred years ago, women were not even permitted to sign a contract or own money in a bank account. The recovery for women to gain equal footing with men is ongoing.

What To Do. We must remember the history of women and particularly the fact that women were once powerful and highly valuable. We must accept females as partners, not slaves, in the evolution of our society. We need to discuss women's history to understand how we got to where we are and what we need to do to shift our culture to once again embrace women and their brilliance. By understanding the evolution of our patriarchal culture, we can begin to untangle our traditions from the truth. We must honor and continue the work of feminists and suffragettes who fought hard to gain basic rights for women. We must admit that even today women do not achieve equality and we must not let our fore-sisters down.

Finally, we must all become feminists – by which I mean both men and women. As Susan Solovic says, "The 'f' word alienates many women because of its association with the bra-burning movement of the early 1970s. If you call a woman a feminist today you may have a fight on your hands. In reality, if you care about the issues that affect your life as a woman, then you are a feminist. But if the label offends you, then forget it. Don't let it deter you from getting involved and taking a position."

Chapter 12

Explore Our Fear of Strong Women

"The reality is that there are still countless numbers of men who do not want to see females achieve and progress. Some believe their position of power is their right and privilege. Others guiltily perceive that it serves their needs to keep women in their place."

~ Nicky Marone

In 2014, the young actress Emma Watson became world famous overnight. Although she had achieved fame as Hermione in the Harry Potter movie series, in September 2014 she rocked the world when she gave a speech at the United Nations on equality for women. As UN Women's Goodwill Ambassador, Watson's campaign, called He4She, beckoned upon men and boys to help women bring about gender equality in the world. As part of her speech, Watson had this to say:

I decided I was a feminist and this seemed uncomplicated to me. But my recent research has shown me that feminism has become an unpopular word. Apparently I am among the ranks of women whose expressions are seen as too strong, too aggressive, isolating, anti-men, and unattractive.

Why is the word such an uncomfortable one? I am from Britain and think it is right that as a woman I am paid the same as my male counterparts. I think it is right that I should be able to make decisions about my own body. I think it is right that women be involved on my behalf in the policies and decision-making of my country. I think it is right that socially I am afforded the same respect as men. But sadly I can say that there is no one country in the world where all women can expect to receive these rights.

Sadly, within minutes of the broadcast of her UN speech Watson was attacked on social media with threats made to distribute nude photos and do all manner of rude and violent physical things to her. This as a result of a speech that very simply asked men to join and support women in a movement to end gender inequality.

An incident such as this is a very real example of the pervasive fear and loathing that exists when strong women express the truth about women's experiences. Some members of our male-centered society view such women as a threat to the status quo that they wish to maintain and so they respond by threatening physical and emotional consequences. This swift and striking response to her speech on social media is a prime example of what women face when they speak up for equality. It says much to explain why many women are frightened to speak out and why even women in power may choose to keep silent on matters of gender inequality.

Sadly, though Watson's women supporters tried to quell the backlash of hate mongering targeted against her by speaking up in support of her speech, their voices were not enough to stop it. Instead the social media backlash and media badgering had to be calmed by hundreds of men (mostly other famous actors) who posted photos of themselves with statements of support for Watson and her cause.

Unfortunately, women who have the courage to speak out about female gender issues who don't have celebrities to back them up are more vulnerable. Consider the case of Anita Sarkeesian, an American media critic, blogger and public speaker who is the founder of Feminist Frequency, a website that exposes and challenges the way in which women are depicted in popular culture. As the *Globe and Mail* reported in July of 2012:

> A woman seeking to expose misogyny in video games has suffered a harsh lesson in the extent of Internet viciousness, as a campaign of harassment escalated to a Canadian man creating a game that let people batter an image of her face.

Anita Sarkeesian, who blogs from California but was born near Toronto and identifies as Canadian-American, had her Wikipedia page locked after it was hacked repeatedly with profanity, lies and pornography. A site on which she fundraises received a concerted campaign to shut her down. And her YouTube channel received a flood of vile messages.

Sarkeesian has also received death threats and there have even been bomb threats at locations where she has been scheduled to speak publicly.

So why as a society do we fear women with power, or women with the power to speak out or act out to try to correct wrongs against women? If we leave the public forum and consider strong female fictional characters (though there aren't so very many), we find that men, by and large, don't like the stories in books or films that feature strong, independent female leads who don't follow the status quo gender role. For instance, mention the movie *Thelma and Louise* and most men get very uncomfortable. Very rarely will it be listed as a man's favorite film. Many wouldn't even bother to see it, let alone like it. It seems there is something unsettling to men about a fictional female character who refuses to accept gender inequality or gender injustice, even when she has every right to take a stand.

Why are characters like Thelma and Louise disturbing to men? Is it because they are treated poorly by men in the story? Does that make men uncomfortable? Or is it that rather than accept the mistreatment, these women do the unthinkable: They take charge and respond to wrongs done to them?

In my opinion, these characters have an impact on men's subconscious causing them to reflect on the truth of gender injustice and the mistreatment of women. They inwardly acknowledge that men have been treating women badly for a long time and that it's not only unfair, but that it's wrong. And they know deep down inside that men have been getting away with it for centuries because society has rendered women powerless to stop it. So a deep fear arises from the idea that this "sleeping giant" might wake up and hold men accountable. This is a very scary thought. I could be wrong, but have you ever wondered why more fathers, husbands and brothers do not stand up for equality? Nor do they necessarily stand behind their daughters and wives when they choose to step up and speak out.

One of the most common ways that society keeps powerful women down is by casting them as evil. One of the best known stories of the evil woman is, of course, the biblical story of Adam and Eve. In this mythical tale of creation, Eve is the first women on earth (born from Adam's rib no less). She and Adam live in an earthly paradise. The way the story unfolds is that Eve is fooled by a snake into biting a fruit from a tree that God has forbidden Adam and Eve to touch. After biting the fruit herself, Eve uses her wiles to convince poor, innocent Adam into taking a bite. This act gets them kicked out of paradise and introduces pain and suffering for all mankind who follow. Eve is depicted as evil because if it weren't for her we'd all still be living in paradise. As you can guess, this is not one of my favorite stories.

Stories like this that depict women as gullible (she speaks to and listens to a snake after all), conniving and evil are abundant in both books and movies and have an extraordinarily powerful impact on our psyches and deepest beliefs about women.

A long line of Disney movies, for instance, follow the pattern of this stereotyping – gullible young women getting into endless trouble, evil witches and horrid step-mothers or royal mothers-in-law who seek to kill rightful heirs to a throne and take over the kingdom. Or here's a good one: an evil wealthy woman who kidnaps puppies because she wants to use their fur to make dog-fur coats. I can't even think of a Disney movie involving a super powerful and strong female role that is likeable and good without being portrayed as desperately lonely or having some type of failing or weakness to keep her in check. Who are our strong female role models in the realm of movies? Is it Angelina Jolie as a super-powerful killing machine?

This stereotype of the evil woman extends to our day-to-day media in very subtle ways. A popular favorite in the news is the rich, evil money-hungry wife. If a woman is powerful she must not only be nasty and selfish, but also desperate for power — usually in the pursuit of fame and money these days, or so we're told by the media. In a newspaper article entitled, "When the Money Goes, So does the Toxic Wife," Tara Winter Wilson of the *Daily Telegraph* talks about toxic wives. These are a group of selfish, money-grubbing women who are emotionally detached and considered a "terrifying species." She says that their sole purpose, besides taking advantage of their rich husbands, is to "shop, lunch and luxuriate." Her research appears to be completely anecdotal and mostly gathered from conversations of recently divorced rich men.

Sometimes it seems we're to believe that unless women are middle class or poor, there' some sort of premeditated swindling or taking advantage of men going on. In her book, *The New Wife*, Susan Shapiro Barash suggests that many women live "pleasurable, struggle-free lives" supported by their rich husbands, which is an inference to me that women with "means" do absolutely nothing. This notion unfortunately propagates the myth that women are lazy and will always try to ride the coattails of their rich husbands if they can find and marry them. I don't know the extent of this scenario, or the validity of it, but I personally know many well-to-do women who work extremely long hours in the volunteer sector contributing to many good causes, earning no money at all. Those women have a poise and a power that is worth writing about.

Fear of powerful women is rooted in our history. For centuries, society did not permit women to have power. Very clear lines were constructed as to what women were permitted to do and women had to live within these strictly defined roles or consequences would result. Women were seen as offering a benefit to society when they abided by what they were allowed to do, but were viewed as dangerous if they did not. A middle ground did not exist.

Women's role was essentially to marry and care for a man and to give birth and care for the man's children. This served men well as it allowed them to have as many children as they could without having to worry about their care. It freed them to work outside of the home while "their women" raised their offspring, thus ensuring their lineage carried forward.

Many of women's traits were frowned upon, criticized as signs of weakness and so dangerous to society that they were condemned outright. These things included anything having to do with female sensuality and sexuality, except, of course, sex for procreation with husbands and pornography for male pleasure. For a period of time even parts of women's bodies were deemed dangerous. A woman's ankles, hair and most particularly breasts were dangerous because they could overwhelm a man's sensibility. This fear still exists today in some cultures that require women to be clothed from head to foot so body parts can't be seen. Education for women was seen as dangerous and prohibited, as it could lead women to leave their role as mothers and care-givers.

And above all, women's intuitive sense and understanding of the earth cycles was particularly dangerous. At one point in history, women were accused of being witches for exhibiting any sign of this and were condemned to death as a result. Burning women (labelled "witches") alive was a practice that actually took place.

The Bottom Line. Society fears powerful women and women who question the status quo of gender inequality. When powerful women speak, our response is to cut them down. We have little respect for powerful women, or at least don't show them the same respect as men. We are often disdainful of wise women and are quick to demonize intrinsically female characteristics of powerful women and label them as weaknesses or put some other negative spin on those traits. Movies, TV and video games readily portray strong (powerful) women as evil villains, crazy bitches, hags, secretly lonely women, psychotic stalkers or helpless victims. Rich and influential women are often labelled as lazy money grabbers, often riding on the coattails of powerful men. We don't acknowledge this fear or hatred for what it is because it is deeply rooted in our history and subconscious beliefs.

What To Do. We need to examine our response to powerful women and women who question the status quo and ask why it is that we fear them. We need to expose the fears as false and change our perceptions of women in power. We need to stop the degrading and diminishing portrayals of women in our society – in media, entertainment, religion and politics. Persistent stereotypes of the sabotaging mother-in-law, the heartless lonely executive, the jealous step-mother, the gold-digging girlfriend and the spineless needy wife need to stop being shoved down our throats. We need to encourage, accept and respect women in power and not label them with negative language that's based on ignorance, fear and hatred. We must educate men and women both to accept women as equal and capable contributors to society. Until we stop fearing women, we will continue to hold them back.

Chapter 13

See the Link Between Power and Violence

"The threat of physical harm is very real for girls and women. Accurate statistics on sexual assaults are difficult to obtain, but all findings indicate an alarming and growing problem in our culture. Various studies estimate that 3.25 to 15 percent of all women will be raped.... Others studies predict that one in four women will be sexually assaulted on university campuses during their college years." ~ Jeanne Elium and Don Elium

Recently, a 30-year-old female jogger was raped one block from my home. I attended the police forum that was held in response where we women learned how to better protect ourselves. We learned about how women are often targets because they are perceived as weak. We were urged to look confident and strong and, if attacked, to strike back.

During the police presentation, a women in the audience asked whether the forum was being held to help the police or to help women. Good question. The officer quite humbly admitted that the police have not done a very good job at helping women to prevent being attacked. Although he said he was committed to changing this, in truth this so-called "crime prevention work," is not really the job of the police. The job of police is simply to enforce the law by finding and prosecuting those who break the law. In our society, it is our governments that create our laws and programs for "public safety." So unless our government thinks that violence against women is an issue of public safety, they're not likely to help women.

I usually avoid talking about women and violence. It hurts too much. I can't read the news about young girls engaged in pornography or the sex trade, which is now a multi-billion dollar industry. I feel completely overwhelmed by the gravity of their circumstances. So, like many women, rather than feel, I shut down and hope someone else with a stronger stomach will do something about it. In her book, *Stitched Up,* Professor Stephanie Vermeulen, notes that the selling of girls and women earns human traffickers $7 billion annually, that 700,000 women are raped annually in the US and that over 50% of the people murdered in India in 1995 were wives murdered by their husbands.

Luckily there are women like Anita Sarkeesian who are emotionally stronger than me and who are willing to take on the fight against violence towards women despite the risk it poses. A few years ago, Sarkeesian, a computer game designer, garnered much media attention when she questioned the depiction of women in video gaming. Although she loved gaming and creating cool games, she was bothered by the endless degrading and sexualized images of women in the games. She decided to conduct some online research in her own community to find out how prevalent it was.

Sarkeesian had barely started her research and sharing early results when she was subjected to attacks on her website and through social media. She was inundated with hate mail and threatened personally. Pictures of her being raped and stabbed were circulated among the gaming community and on social media. Women around the world were so outraged they spoke up in her defense. Soon enough she had a massive following and was successful in crowdfunding her research. Even though she is famous, however, she cannot speak publicly without requiring security guards! Most recently, there have been bomb threats to facilities where she has been scheduled to speak. And her crime was simply addressing the negative representation and role of female characters in gaming!

All violence against women is so very appalling in any format, yet why are there so many video games, movies and books that involve the torturing of women? How can we call ourselves an advanced society when some husbands regularly beat their wives and there are places in the world where men make a living by kidnapping and selling women and girls to other men? Why do we have hundreds of rape-relief centers and homes to protect women and children from violent husbands/fathers? Why are these centers so grossly under-funded?

Gender expert Jackson Katz suggests that men continue to be raised in a way that confuses masculinity with aggression. As a result, boys grow up with the old "John Wayne" model of manhood in their minds supporting the idea that they can be cold, aggressive and mean to women. Here are a few of the statistics that concern him most:

- Males are the victims and perpetrators in 90% of homicides.

- 90% of people who commit violent physical assault are men.

- Men perpetuate 95% of all serious domestic violence.

- Of those in prison that have been found guilty of rape, 98.8% are male.

- An estimated one in four men will use violence against his partner in his life time.

Violence against women is clearly a huge societal issue, yet it is rarely mentioned. Even Stephen Harper, the former Prime Minister of Canada, recently said that the killing of hundreds of Canadian Aboriginal women was not a societal issue. In his opinion, these hundreds of murders were simply single crimes happening in individual circumstances that can be best dealt with through the criminal process. Last year in Nigeria hundreds of girls were kidnapped by a terrorist group called Boko Haram and have yet to be located. How can governments with military and special police forces not be able to locate 200 girls? Why is it not their priority?

Our society can't seem to admit that violence against women is actually culturally supported. We refuse to admit that there is an uneven power dynamic between men and women, individually and structurally, and that it's the power imbalance that is directly related to violence against women. Not only do we fail to acknowledge this, but we tolerate this violence by downplaying its impact, and even reinforce the tolerance through regular sensationalizing of violence in movies and television and the normalization of pornography.

Indeed, when women experience violence we often think it's a personal problem with an overly-aggressive spouse and in some cases we even blame women by suggesting that they provoked an attack or were "asking for it." I often wonder whether we as a society would do more about this type of violence if it were violence experienced by young boys or helpless men.

So why don't more women do anything to stop this violence? In my second year of law school my criminal law professor, Constance Backhouse, answered this question by engaging our class in an exercise. We were asked to find out why wives who were beaten by their husbands refused to bring charges against them for "wife assault" and to come up with a solution. We quickly discovered that women who were beaten were deeply ashamed, often had no money and were afraid of their partners, often for the duration of their lives. We also learned that our criminal law system not only was unable to protect them, but was ineffective at both holding these men accountable and preventing attacks in the future. Indeed, in many instances the criminal system actually made matters worse!

Many people blame women for not getting away from violent husbands, telling them to stand up for their rights. We do not realize that it's not women who are to blame, but rather a society that tolerates this and a legal system that clearly cannot protect women. After learning this, our law class decided to create a brochure for abused women so they could at least learn how to sue their husbands for assaulting them in the civil (not criminal) system. At least this way these women might get money so they could leave a bad situation.

I can't tell you how many times I hear people blaming women for "jogging after dark" and engaging in other risky behaviors like parking in underground parking lots or dressing "inappropriately." It's quite insulting to demand that our daughters cover every inch of their bodies to avoid being seen as attracting violence. Yet this is exactly what we do in our current culture. We refuse to admit that the problem is men harming women and that this harm comes about because men have the power to do so. We dare not call it a "male" or a "power" issue, but, until we do, the problem will not go away.

But, before we blame men, it is critical to step back and see what's really going on. Although men are the perpetrators of many crimes against women, males in our society are part of a larger system that needs to be scrutinized. In this system, we do not take violence against women very seriously. In this system, women have very little power relative to men and, in this system, we have institutions (such as our justice system and marriage) that maintain power imbalances between men and women.

The best example of an imbalanced system is our family structure that essentially expects women to raise children and become financially dependent on husbands, making it financially impossible to leave a relationship if violence does occur. Marital violence is deeply intertwined with financial power, with the person wielding the financial power often taking the role of the aggressor. But we refuse to see this reality. Here is an excerpt from my book, *Motherhood is Madness*:

> When a woman marries and has children she may give up her career and become financially dependent on her husband. This comes at a huge cost to women and their families. Women lose income and the sense of security that provides. They lose not just jobs but entire careers and the investment in their own skills and experience

that would provide later opportunities. They lose money, insurance and savings even if they leave for a short while. Mothers rarely get back to where they would have been had they not taken the time off. In effect, mothers are investing in their husbands' careers at the expense of their own. And should a women divorce she will likely be in a worse financial situation than her husband.

Part of the reason we cannot admit this is because gender inequality and women's lack of power is such a very large issue. We look away. Because it's so prevalent, it's acceptable. Also we dare not admit that women who get beat up by their husbands do not have authority or power because such an acknowledgement might cause us to look inward and examine our own lives, where, as women, we too have very little power, and, as men, we don't want to admit to the disparity in power. Can you imagine saying to your husband, "I found out today why men beat their wives. It's because they can. And the reason they can is because women are physically weaker and will not stand up to them because of that fact and because they simply don't have power in the relationship in other ways, financially, emotionally, and psychologically; nor do they have a support system or a legal system that they can count on."

To compound matters, because women are underrepresented in government, they are unable to bring about changes to laws or education that would prevent things like gender discrimination, sexism and violence against women. Women, and particularly those who are in abusive situations, literally often do not have the time, interest, money or ability to change things, so they have little impact on a society that is only willing to fund a few safe temporary shelters here and there.

The Bottom Line. In our society women suffer way too much violence — from beatings to rapes and murder. Because we pretend it's an individual as opposed to a societal issue, we do not deal with it properly. We blame women or accuse "bad" men and rely on the police and criminal laws that actually often cause the abused women even more harm without addressing the real problem. We think that wife-beating and attacks on girls and women are random, remote or individual when this is simply not true.

The truth is that violence against women is caused not just by aggressive men, but by women's basic lack of power in their relationships and in society generally. By not paying attention to this lack of power we actually accept and support violence in many ways, including in our families and in our violent media.

What To Do. We should be ashamed as a society and we need to take action to stop violence against women immediately. We must stop blaming women and individual men and must look at a systemic problem in our whole society that keeps women powerless. We must stop thinking that our criminal system will help and admit that it often can cause more harm.

We must stop pretending that violence against women is a small issue and must own up to the truth that as a society we not only tolerate it, we promote it — through mainstream media such as advertisements, television programing, movies, music videos, video gaming and Internet streaming that promote and encourage the notion that men should have power over women in whatever manner they like, physical, financial, psychological and emotional. We must recognize the fact that gender-based violence is due to women having little power, influence or value. If we are not revolted by it, we may be contributing to it.

Chapter 14

Ensure Women Participate in Daily News

"Part of the reason for all this inequity is that women still aren't well represented working in the media. According to the American Society of Newspaper editors, they make up only 37 percent of reporters at daily newspapers. They're just 24 percent of television writers, directors and producers. And the major network news shows have women as on-air experts on 13 percent of the time (even in stories about women or girls)." ~ Catherine Dee

When Anita Roddick, the owner of the cosmetic company Body Shop International, died in 2007, her obituary was not on the front page of our national newspaper. Although she was perhaps the most successful female entrepreneur of this generation and her bath and body products were and continue to be in almost every home in North America, she was also well-known as a human rights activist and environmental campaigner. Despite her very significant presence as a leader, she barely made it onto page five. At the time, I wondered, "Who made the decision to place the story there?" I still wonder on a daily basis, where are all the stories about women? Are women doing nothing "newsworthy?"

Everyday millions of people watch the news on television or read the news in papers and online. Because we rely so heavily on this facet of the media to provide us with stories of the events in the world, it's important to notice how the news as a medium ignores and impacts women.

Research shows that women are not only often absent from news stories, but are also absent from the higher offices within the organizations preparing and producing the news. As a rule, women tend to play only minor roles as producers, directors and even journalists. Rarely are they "heavy hitters" to adopt a popular sports term. The news media industry is very much a man's world and it's holding women back in a big way by underrepresentation in the industry and story angles that often perpetuate stereotypical notions of women.

What kinds of news stories involve women? If you look closely at newspapers, listen to the radio or watch television you will discover a few things about women and girls in the media. First, as previously noted, you will find that there are fewer females in the presentation of the news. Second, you will find that when news stories involve women, they are primarily softhearted stories, often about distraught or upset mothers or about women as victims. On occasion you will find stories about a handful of very powerful women – women leaders, politicians and famous actresses. But what you may not notice right away is that all of these women are described in sexist and stereotypical ways, with references and sometimes the sole focus being their hair styles, their "look," not uncommonly their size and their clothing.

The vast majority of news is, quite frankly, about men. This fact reinforces the idea that only men are important or relevant as far as news is concerned. While women are less frequently in the public eye, men are in it endlessly because they hold more positions of power in corporations, governments, religious institutions, the entertainment industry and more. Women would like to be there in similar numbers to represent, but it's still not the case. Ultimately, the damaging message that we all hear loud and clear is that women are not newsworthy. And so the problem perpetuates.

Another fact that tilts news in favor of men, however, has to do with the world of journalism and those who report and write about the news. Here's a short list of "journalism" realities:

- Most of the "important" news stories are reported by male reporters.

- News is often reported from a male perspective, reporting on men for men.

- Very few women are in the news and rarely interviewed as experts.

- Women are less likely to be hired as news anchors; more often hired to be weather or local events reporters (i.e., with less status).

To compound matters, journalists often describe women in less-than-flattering ways. Often they focus on age, marital status and the personal lives of women. Is she old? Is she fat? Does she have a rich father or rich husband? Unlike men, women's credentials are not found in university degrees or work experience, but rather in beauty and their relationships to men in power. When women do appear in the news, they are often standing behind their powerful husbands or colleagues. The standard photo is of four or five men in grey and black with one token woman, wearing a colored blazer. The other impression often given is that strong women stand alone and are therefore lonely. For example, to use a powerful female from British politics, do you know what Margaret Thatcher's husband looked like? Do you know if she had any children?

Unfortunately, the most common news stories on women relate to violence, murder and prostitution. In these situations, women are portrayed as helpless or in need of (male) assistance. Even in gender-neutral news stories of tragedy, such as the aftermath of hurricanes, floods or earthquakes, more often than not the images are of women and children in despair, more rarely men in despair.

As for news about sports, about 90% of sports news is about male sports, and in North America that means heavy on the hockey, baseball, basketball, football and soccer. The bulk of the sports depicted are so removed from women's lives that a large percentage of women don't read about or watch sports in the media. The sad reality is that when women's sports *are* covered, the women are the least "covered" insofar as their sports attire is concerned, and the focus tends to be on their clothing and their physical appearance. Think of the two most popular women sports given media attention, particularly on TV: figure-skating and gymnastics (and more recently women's tennis with lots about what the Williams' sisters are wearing). Imagine the flack if we reported on male bodies and male sports attire in the same manner.

On any given day, at any given time, the events that become the "news" of the day are just a fraction of the events that occur in the world; and this fraction doesn't reflect women equally or fairly. This slice of reality is selected by a few people as being relevant for a particular newspaper or program. In essence, producers and editors around the world decide what we, the general public, will read or see as "news." To my mind, this is why we have so much violence reported in the news. Editors, mostly men, think that violence is newsworthy and that reporting on it will attract more viewers or readers.

Those in the media will likely argue that they are just meeting the demands of their audience in both regular news, as well as sports news. If this is truly the case, since men seem to be, by and large, their main audience, news agencies continue to cater to male needs and wants. Male-dominated sports and news of war and aggression supposedly peak their interests. The more news in this vein that they publish, the more men will read and view that news. This tendency marginalizes women and keeps them at arms' length from engaging in current events. So the question that needs to be asked and addressed is: How do we create news that reflects women's lives and women's concerns when those selecting the news and buying the news are predominantly men?

The Bottom Line. The daily news is problematic for women. First of all, the news is rarely about women, which suggests that their activities are not newsworthy. Second, the producers of the news are rarely women and third, when women are portrayed in the news it is rarely in a supportive or flattering way. Powerful and/or strong women are infrequently featured in the news and when they are they are often described or portrayed in less than positive ways, with language that praises or plays up their looks and attire and thereby under-emphasizes and devalues their actual and valid accomplishments.

What To Do. We need to examine media outlets and ask ourselves: Who sits on the Board of Directors? How many women are there in leadership and editorial positions? Do male leaders in the industry have a balanced perspective on women? Are they "equality-minded?" Do they have a way of ensuring that women are properly represented in the news and participate fully in producing the news? It's important that we hold those who produce the news accountable. It's paramount that we see female representation in the media at all levels so that women are seen to "matter" and that women's voices and stories are heard.

Part Three

A Male-Female Partnership

Chapter 15

Understand What True Equality Means

"If I ask if they believe that men and women should have equal rights, they say yes. When I ask if their schools are sexist, they are likely to say no. But if I ask if they have ever been harassed sexually at their school, they say yes and tell me stories. If I ask who writes most of the material they study at school, they know its men. If I ask them who is more likely to be a principal, they say a man. If I ask who has more power, they say men." ~ Mary Pipher

It is important to understand the true definition of equality if our goal is to place women and men on equal footing. Given the rhetoric around equality it's surprising we can keep these concepts straight.

A male friend of mine who is now a surgeon told me a story that highlights the difficulty we all have in understanding true equality. In his high-stress residency years a female medical student had asked for special permission to sleep at her home rather than the hospital when she was on call. She had two children at home and was nursing a baby. The supervising doctor refused the request on the grounds that doing so would not be fair to the other residents. As a result, even though she was seen in the group to be the doctor with the most potential and the highest grades, she quit her residency and decided not to pursue surgery since, as she told her colleagues, it was too demanding.

This example highlights the difference between equal treatment and real equality. In this situation, the supervising doctor did not treat this female equitably. Although he did what most people would do and simply applied the rules in the same manner to everyone, the results proved disastrous to the woman.

It took me years to understand why this felt so wrong. I mean didn't he treat everyone equally? Like many brilliant lawyers who've spent years arguing before judges and governments, I knew this narrow definition was not acceptable.

The supervising doctor was not in the position to question a brutal system of residency. Indeed, since he was engrained in the system he did not even notice that the 24/7 sleep-at-the hospital system was causing women to quit. He simply wanted to be fair by applying the rules equally to everyone. Most people think that this is equality, but it is not. The reason his decision does not feel right is because we only look at individuals and do not look at the whole system.

He thought that giving a nursing mother a break would mean treating her "favorably." Yet, because he did not do this, he prevented this doctor from having the opportunity to have a career in surgery. If we step back we will see a tightly-constructed process for entry into our medical profession. Like the process for many professions, medicine is a highly competitive, dog-eat-dog system that does not allow anyone who is unwilling to work 24/7 to succeed. We have created a structure so demanding of time and energy that women are hard-pressed to make their way in. Not so for men, as their role outside of work does not make the same demands on their time. When it comes to marriage and family, men can still give the bulk of their attention to work and have someone else take care of serious commitments and obligations on the home front.

Is it necessary that every single doctor sleep overnight in a hospital during residency? If we force all doctors to abandon their entire non-working lives for their residency, what kind of doctor are we likely to attract? Furthermore, by requiring this rigid, overnight requirement, what kind of people are we rejecting, and perhaps even expecting to fall out of the loop?

If we really wanted women to succeed we would create a completely flexible system that would work for everyone, not just men. Because women's lives are different than men's lives, both require different things. Equal pay for equal work is obvious for both. However, by requiring that everyone work 100 hours a week in order to get promoted, it's inevitable that a disproportionate number of women will suffer a setback because they may choose or simply "need" to do volunteer work in the home or elsewhere. Men will not suffer the same setback.

The word equality means equal opportunity in action, not just words. So to be acting equitably it would make sense to make sure that women can have the same opportunities to move forward as men. Those women who leave high-paying jobs to take on responsibilities with children or aging parents at home should not suffer barriers to returning to work or experience significant losses in pay and status when they do return.

Today, the legal definition of equality means equal in results, not just on face value. It means considering the impact on women (e.g., does it keep women out of jobs); the impact on the profession (e.g., does it keep females out of the medical profession); and the impact on our society (e.g., does it prevent women from being educated and financially independent)? If the supervising doctor had considered these factors I am sure he would have found a way to accommodate the female resident without upsetting any of the other residents.

Equality can only be achieved when people understand that we actually created all of our systems – from the medical to the family system – and that they were and still are based on men's needs. We can choose to create systems that support both women and men in having full lives and families or not. We can choose to make it impossible for women to have a career and a family at the same time or not. If we care about women and other human beings, we would choose equality.

The Bottom Line. Most people think that if we treat women the same as men, we are treating them equitably, but this is not true. This equal treatment has been shown to cause women to suffer disproportionally because the rules and systems we are working within impact women and men differently.

Many institutions, like the medical training model, often impair women's ability to succeed and it's this harm that indicates that the system is not working. Equity comes about when women and men are treated fairly, given their circumstances. It means creating a world and institutions where people are treated fairly so that everyone has equal opportunity.

What To Do. We must understand that treating men and women the same way does not necessarily guarantee equality. Instead we need to look at our corporations and other systems and discover how their basic structure and rules keep women out or keep them perpetually at the bottom. The easiest way to think about equality is this: Does this way of doing things prevent females from doing things that males can do? Are the rules that we've created unfairly giving advantage to men? If so, do we want this to continue or is there a better way to ensure equality? We can actually choose as a society to build systems that allow both genders to live full lives or not.

Chapter 16

Embrace Devine Feminine Power

"The kind of power that women need is not ruthless, controlling, self-serving, domination-seeking power – power without benefit of love. It is not staying up by keeping others down. What we need is a potent, forceful power, yes, but one that is also compassionate, that enables others as well." ~ Sue Monk Kidd

Women tend to shy away from the topic of power. They feel embarrassed mentioning it. When I first told my closest friend that I was writing a book on helping women gain power, status and money, she laughed out loud. When she realized that I was absolutely serious, she said this, "Really, Maureen, do you think that power is what women really want? Is that what *you* really want?"

This got me thinking. Don't women want power? They most definitely want freedom. They also want control over their lives and security and some sense of predictability. Women tell me that they want a comfortable life, a healthy family and love, but for some reason they don't make the link between attaining those things and power. Not only that, many women will say outright that they do not want power! To me this means that they either don't understand the importance of power or, if they do, are too afraid to admit that they know about the importance of power and actually want it.

From conversations with female friends and family, it occurs to me that for most women the word "power" is a loaded one. It causes problems for two main reasons. First, for some women, claiming to want power feels generally inappropriate or wrong and, second, many women often find the word and the whole concept of power aggressive and distasteful. In my book *Lean Out,* I explain the reasons why women today are ambivalent about power and often fear it:

> Although women need power and want power, they both fear it and avoid using it. This is because as a society we not only teach girls to shun power we actively encourage them to give it away. We are told that we must always put others first and must never appear more important or powerful than a man. We reinforce these messages by shaming women who display powerful behaviors, calling them pushy, bossy or bitchy and by treating the most powerful women in harshly critical ways, and holding them to the highest standards. Women who dare to have intelligence, money, status and power – or use it – take a very big risk. We should not be surprised when most women shrink and hide when the word "power" is raised. By teaching women to avoid, fear and refrain from using their power we hold them back.

This aversion to women holding power is described in detail in the book, *Shadow King,* by psychologist Sidra Stone. Stone suggests that deep inside our unconscious minds resides a so-called "Inner Patriarch" that holds the traditional beliefs from a time when men were all powerful and women submissive. This inner voice tells women that they should not assume positions of power in the world. As Stone says, "This objection to women in power runs very, very deep. It almost feels cellular, as though it has been programmed into our DNA."

For many women the word "power" itself conjures up images of control, domination and violence. This makes complete sense given that our human history has become synonymous with using power to keep people down in order to keep other people up. Indeed, our entire history is filled with extraordinary violence and utter abuses of power. Just think of all the wars and how few examples we have of people using power in a more positive manner like Mahatma Gandhi or Martin Luther King.

The word power carries with it even more disturbing connotations. Women have not only been the target of aggressive power, often being kept as slaves in their homes, but they've also been used as tools of war, primarily through the horror of rape, though through witch burnings as well. It should come as no surprise that the topic of power is distasteful and disturbing to so many women.

This type of power is called "power-over" or dominance-based power. It implies one person or group is using their power to control another. This understanding of power originates in a very ancient world view that conquering others is necessary to survive. Such an assessment often feels foreign and even offensive to women. It is not in any sense a feminine version of power.

One of the biggest difficulties for women in reclaiming power is wrestling with the word itself and understanding what real feminine power is. Although we don't give much thought to what our feminine version might look like, to reclaim the word as feminine is necessary and the word most definitely cannot be feared, or considered inappropriate, for women to use.

Feminine power is best seen as "power-within" or "power in relation." In this way, power does not mean dominance, but rather "empowerment." At an individual level, this means tapping each person's inner strengths and as a group it means tapping the strength of the group as a whole, otherwise known as relational power. These types of power look very similar to the modern concepts of emotional intelligence, which means knowing and managing yourself, and social intelligence, which means being able to relate with others. This type of power, of self and in relation, is rarely used for aggression and it never involves harming others. This power is less a "head-sense" or mental dominating power and more a "heart-felt," body-based power.

This deep feminine power relates closely to and includes sensing and intuition, female traits that have largely been ignored and/or degraded in our society. As a rule, we have elevated the masculine qualities such as directness and decisiveness. So for women to step into their truest power, they must not only own these "lost" strengths, but more importantly, find the deepest source of power that all women own.

In their book, *Raising a Daughter,* Jeanne Elium and Don Elium suggest that there are some biologically-based differences that reflect female strengths and make them most unique and valuable. They suggest that at the most basic level females see life as a circle, not a hierarchy. They therefore value connection to all and to the cycles of life. Females also behave as vessels for life, as child bearers, caregivers and nurturers. Women and girls are also sensitive to smell, taste, touch and hidden messages and are communicative with strong language skills. They are considered the holders of relationships.

Wendy Shalit, in *Girls Gone Mild,* writes about how the media has convinced women and girls that their main source of power is their sexuality. Sadly, instead of honoring it and elevating it as something beautiful, we are taught that getting drunk, taking off your clothes and having casual sex are indicators of empowerment. Rather than encouraging women to take back their sensuality and powerful bodies, however, Shalit promotes abstinence, non-wildness and urges girls to stay at home! She wrongly blames feminism (with much vengeance, unfortunately) and oppresses girls further by limiting their freedoms, again.

In a world that honors the feminine, there would be no such thing as showing too much compassion. Those who feel the urge to meet others' needs should be supported in doing so. A culture that values relationships would:

- Value friends and time spent together.

- Trust people and believe they have good intentions.

- Show gratitude and say please and thank you.

- Have more parties, celebrations and community events.

- Smile because we want to – not because we have to make others feel good.

- Conduct research to help define what is truly feminine.

- Re-tell the feminine myths...women need to tell their own stories.

- Create new role models of strong and feminine women.

As Elium says, "If I could give my daughter one thing, I would give her a world that valued the personhood of women, understanding that creative work in the community is as necessary to her feminine soul as nurturing children and/or creating a home."

If women are truly to be powerful and whole, we cannot simply act like men and adopt their ways of gaining power. We must embrace our feminine side. No matter how powerful a woman might feel, without access to her deep feminine strengths she will always feel only partly grounded and powerful.

The deepest sense of feminine "knowing" is called the Devine Feminine. Sue Monk Kidd refers to it as the feminine soul: "When I use the term the feminine soul, I'm referring to a women's inner repository of the Devine Feminine, her deep sources, her natural instinct, guiding wisdom, and power. It is everything that keeps a woman powerful and grounded within herself, complete in herself, belonging to herself, and yet connected to all that is. Connection with this inner reality is a woman's most priceless experience."

Here are two great perspectives on feminine power.

- "Female concepts of power focus on sharing, on making connections. They aren't self-centered; they are not about heroic egos. Powerful women do not talk about dramatic rescues or single-handed triumphs. Instead the ideas of power that we enjoy are non-hierarchical and highly participatory. They are about us, not me." (Margaret Heffernan)

- "Female power transcends what are known politically as women's issues. Female power has to do with women taking an active part in the conversation – whether in the public arena or at the dinner table – and having the same emotional space in which to do it as men. It means women not having to fear punishment of any kind. It means women not having to worry that they'll be considered unfeminine if they speak up." (Marianne Williamson)

Although we women know on some level what it means to be authentically female or feminine, much of this knowledge is buried quite deep. We know for example that honoring the entire world and our connection with it is a feminine strength, yet we don't want to claim it often because we either don't know how, or we fear it. Sue Monk Kidd suggests that females enter "the deep sleep" in their early teens. They lose their sense of self and with it their feisty spirit.

Too many women today fear that if they show their own true self they will be rejected, or worse they'll remain on our cultural treadmill feeling that they are never good enough, not pleasing enough and not living up to the sanctioned model of the feminine.

> **The Bottom Line.** Women avoid the word power for two reasons, we are taught that it's not appropriate for us to hold power or be powerful and also because the word power conjures up for us images of control, domination and violence. Because of this women do not realize that they have rejected not only their claim to power, but also the type of power that is at the core of their beings: divine feminine power.

What To Do. We must stop discouraging girls and women from holding or wielding power. We must teach them about the importance of power and how it plays out in women's lives. We need to reclaim and embrace the concept of feminine power. This means acknowledging that feminine strengths such as intuition and caring have been historically devalued and turning to those who understand the concept of the Devine Feminine and feminine knowing. As Marianne Williamson writes, "Only when women go into the world to express an authentic balance of intelligence with compassion, representing not only women but the effort within all human beings to retrieve our lost hearts, will there be genuine liberation of the imprisoned Goddess."

Chapter 17

Engage Men and Boys

"Men...by virtue of their status as gatekeepers and power brokers in organizations possess as a group, inherent structural advantages over women. As for women, as a group, to break the glass ceiling depends on the extent to which men are prepared to work with them as equals, offering them the same types of informal as well as formal supports that men have themselves historically relied on for advancement. For this to happen, men have to assume an active role as equal teammates and allies of women, which requires identifying compelling reasons to do so."

~ Mark Maier

Every time I buy a book on empowering women I ask myself, "Why are women the ones who must work so hard to make the world better? Why don't men realize the need as a society to have women fully engaged in the world? Why do we have to convince men that women deserve basic human fairness?

Most people think that men don't feel the pain of inequality as much as women and thus are unlikely to take action. Others believe that men benefit from the subjugation of women so do not desire to change a good thing. As Susan Solovic says, "What incentive do men have to change when they are the ones in control?" I, however, always come back to this: Men, like women, are living in the same prison. Men are controlled by the same culture and its institutions that we are all living in. Although this prison appears to have harsher impacts on women, it is inconsistent with our survival on this planet.

Indeed, the culture that holds women back is the same one that holds back men and prevents men from taking action. Men, like women, are caught on a treadmill that they cannot see. They know that they are running way too fast, but do not know how to stop the insanity.

For example, when a husband says he has to work late, he actually must work late. He does not really have a choice because if he did not, he might get fired. In the corporate system that we have created he feels he is essentially forced to choose work over his family. He might very well prefer to go home to have a nice dinner with his family, but he does not. As a result, his family is upset, but accepts it as the price they all must pay to be able to live a comfortable life.

Although men benefit in many ways from our systems, the gains are mostly short term. In the long term, a system that cannot accommodate all humans is not sustainable. Whether from inside or outside, the system will begin to crack and fall apart. For men and women both, being enslaved to the system is difficult and it's one of the main reasons the divorce rate is above 50%. Only rare families can survive under the demands of our current system.

In this prison, men may have more comfortable chairs and a few slaves, but in my opinion, the true happiness of all humans can never be achieved until each and every one of us is free. So if men think things are just fine, perhaps they do not understand how good things could truly be. Until we deal with the prison, we are all prisoners. We are all worse off until we break free.

But how can men help? If you look to history you will see a few distinct phases relating to women's advancement. The first phase was to simply reject women and keep them out of employment. The second was to include them, but only to the extent they were skilled in the masculine model. In most cases this involved "fixing" women. Phase three involved creating policies and practices for equal opportunity. This included maternity leaves and equal pay legislation. The benefits of all of these phases are now evident. We have more women at work; we have a robust economy.

We are now at stage four where we are just beginning to truly appreciate the value of women. We no longer want to separate and degrade certain work as "women's work" because we see this work as useful to our whole society. We are beginning to see women's feminine strengths as valuable and necessary to the evolution of the whole planet. We are seemingly on the cusp of accepting (or at least some of us are on this cusp), without a sense of jealousy or competition, that we truly need women to be free. We see occasional glimpses of men willing to work as partners with women and gradually (though still slowly) some men feeling less intimidated by powerful women.

As we evolve, we realize that we all share the same needs: we all need love, happiness and freedom. However, as long as half of the population (women) is unhappy or feel unjustly treated by inequality, the other half (men) will never truly be happy.

Professors Debra Meyerson and Robin Ely suggest that we need to advance women through a two-pronged approach. In their article, "Using Difference to Make a Difference," they suggest that we continue to tear down the obvious systemic barriers that hold women back. This would both advance women and reap the benefit of their diverse knowledge and experience.

At the same time we must change the "process" of the system. We must create a more organic and less hierarchical structure that at its core is continuous evolution and learning. In such a system, people are encouraged to fully engage in ways that permit them to question even the most basic manner in which we do things. As they say, "In the course of these interactions, the organizations, norms, values and practices are open to scrutiny, providing the necessary impetus to question and challenge traditional beliefs, including those that legitimize inequalities."

This shift in systems is slowly occurring inside some corporations. Not surprising, the modern systems are the ones that appeal most to women, as described here by Helen Fisher: "Corporations are changing from hierarchical structures where leaders command from on high to laterally connected webs where managers favor team playing, egalitarian connections, consensus, and flexibility. Although both men and women unquestionably possess all of these traits, such ways of thinking and behaving are more characteristic of women."

In addition to structural change, men must make a change at an attitudinal level. As boys they were programmed to be tough guys. This meant denying their vulnerability and acting out aggressively. It also meant dominating others. Educator Anita Roberts suggests that this social conditioning causes many men to act in somewhat violent ways and abuse their power. Although as a society, we have come to accept this as the norm, it's time to turn this narrow gender-raising on its head.

In order to do this, men must learn about the impact of their actions and must be open to adopting a more humane way of interacting with the world. Many groups of men are emerging to help men do this work such as the Good Man Project. This is not an exercise to feminize men. It is an attempt to de-program men. The best documentary to watch on this topic is called "Tough Guise," a documentary by Jackson Katz of the Media Education Center. It shows how we teach males to behave badly and assert dominance. Here are a few examples of dominant behaviors that we tolerate and promote in boys:

- Speaking loudly and yelling.
- Interrupting or talking overtop of another.
- Standing too close and taking up physical space.
- Inappropriate touching.

- Not admitting to mistakes or not knowing something.

- Being tough and insensitive to others.

- Pushing, hitting and standing over others.

You will notice that women and girls are taught the exact opposite of these behaviors. Indeed, these actions are considered taboo, unfeminine and aggressive when exhibited by women.

Related to this attitude of dominance and aggression is the attitude of privilege and entitlement. In his book, *Making Love, Playing Power,* author Ken Dolan-Del Vecchio describes how being a male meant that he was privileged and this entitled him to better treatment than girls. He suggests that boys and men must start to recognize this entitlement before they can truly help women.

The Bottom Line. Men and boys obviously play a critical role in creating a world where women and girls are free to be who they want to be, yet rarely are they called upon to act. They are not only fathers and brothers, but boyfriends and bosses. They are in positions of power in corporations and government where they are able to influence change. All men are being held back by the same prison that women are, they just don't realize it.

What To Do. We must all want women to be powerful. It's that simple. If men and women truly care about their mothers, sisters and daughters they should find many ways to ensure equal distribution of power. This means challenging the whole system, our own personal biases and the institutions we work within, especially corporate and religious institutions. Men must be willing to be true partners at both home, at work and in society.

Chapter 18

Use Language that Includes Women

"Language builds pictures in our minds. These pictures when repeated often enough, build expectation. These expectations affect what we do, what we aspire to do, and how we treat others who do not conform to our expectations." ~ Selma Greenberg

The English language is essentially a male-based language. Indeed most of our modern languages were formalized by male scholars and until about 150 years ago anything scholarly necessarily excluded women from its ranks. In addition, because women were not permitted to participate in public affairs such as voting or holding government offices, there is a general absence of women in the written word in the English language. It did not occur to the drafters of our laws and constitutions, for example, that women be included in the text. Or, it occurred to them, but they purposefully left women out as a measure to devalue them.

Our English language and the language of business, economics and politics are male-based. This means not only that texts were written solely by males, but also that terminology and referencing reflects only the experiences of those who were in power at the time – men. This is why so many of our history books do not include very many references to women. Women were not permitted in the public sphere so were not really visible and the domestic sphere was deemed not worth writing about. Those who wrote all our laws and constitutions were also entirely men and did not consider women to be worthy to participate in creating these texts or indeed to be include in these texts.

Not including women in language is a wrong that hopefully continues to be set right. Referencing only men or exclusively using the pronoun "he" in the past was another way to take women out of the picture and was a purposeful acknowledgement that women didn't matter. The practice *should* no longer exist; however, many schools still rely on texts that are solely male-centered and, unfortunately, many publishers of current school and university texts feel that it's sufficient to simply use the "he" pronoun when referring to both males and females. I have often wondered how different the world would be if we instead used the "she" pronoun to describe both men and women. It is empowering to be included in the written word and "he" simply doesn't cut it for empowering and including girls and women.

In her book, *A Girls' Guide to Life,* Catherine Dee questions why "Peace on Earth and Goodwill toward Men" couldn't have read "Peace on Earth and Goodwill to All." She says, "Male-centered language makes children picture just males in the same way that female-centered language makes them picture just females. Words and phrases such as cameraman and every man for himself make women and girls seem insignificant. And language that excludes part of a population also has a negative impact on the groups' collective self-image."

Dee makes another valid observation about language when she writes, "feminists have other beefs with the English language, notably vocabulary. Hundreds of English words referring to females have negative connotations, such as sissy, which is derived from sister; and sexual connotations such as slut. By contrast there aren't many words referring to males, and those that exist don't have the same negative punch." Here's a short list I've come up with of slang terms that are regularly aimed at women: bitch, ball breaker, slut, cunt, ho, snob, frump, princess, brainiac, husband snatcher, cougar, fat girl, vamp, boobalicious, yummy mummy, MILF, uptight, cold fish, virgin, cock-tease, am-bitchous and beauty queen. Imagine what it feels like to be on the receiving end of these words. It's both embarrassing and crushing.

Though not as harsh as the words on the above list, consider how many times women are called "girls" or "ladies." Consider the following exercise:

> Close your eyes. Now imagine a room full of girls and describe what you see. What are they doing? What are they wearing? Let that image go and now imagine a room full of ladies. Now describe what you see and what the gents are doing. What are they wearing? Now let that second image go and imagine a room full of women. What do you see? For most people the three images should be completely different. They are likely to see children when asked to describe the girls; grandmothers when asked to describe ladies and a wide range of women when asked to describe women. Language causes one to conjure up images in one's head and these images can limit or expand one's thinking about the value of the person or thing that is referenced.

What is perhaps more harmful, however, is not just the words that are hurled at women, but the frequency with which they're used and the tolerance society has for their usage. Rarely do I hear a man or a woman suggesting that using the word "bitch" is not appropriate. And the cost of this silence to women is massive. Without even realizing it, girls and women live in fear of being put down or rejected by both men and women with these labels. It not only feels bad; it stays with us and impacts our self-esteem.

As a result of the use of language, simple words can become powerful, yet seemingly invisible tools to keep females "in their place" and to strip them of power. And we wonder why women suffer from low self-esteem and depression.

The Bottom Line. Our language is male-based. This means that it was written by males and tends to reflect the male experience. It not only excludes women, but includes many worlds that reflect outdated stereotypes and negative views of women (e.g., slut and bitch). Even the attempt to use Ms as a gender neutral term has been met with resistance.

What To Do. Stop thinking our language is neutral. It is not. Work on finding and using words that are inclusive and respectful of both men and women. Here are a few examples of gender neutral terms: ballet dancer rather than ballerina; building owner rather than landlord; chairperson rather than chairman; homemaker rather that housewife; handmade rather than man made; staffing rather than manning; cleaner rather than cleaning lady; police officer rather than policeman.

Chapter 19

Create an Occupy Women Movement

"A woman in Deep Sleep is one who goes about in an unconscious state. She seems unaware or unfazed by the truth of her own female life, the truth about women in general, the way women and the feminine have been wounded, devalued and limited within cultures, churches and families. She cannot see the wound or feel the pain." ~ Sue Monk Kidd

A few [men] actually believe that females are inferior. Still others perpetuate the concept of natural subservience of women. Some simply fear change. Whatever the reason, the result is the same – a world against which your daughter must fortify herself if she is to overcome the narrow, ignorant prejudices of those who would use their power and authority to obstruct her path. Consequently, it must be the job of those who believe in the development of female talent to create a world willing and able to accept feminine contributions. ~ Nicky Marone

At this point you may be asking yourself, why is it taking so long for women to advance in our society and in the world generally.

There are three main reasons why things have not improved much for women. First, women can't see it. This is not their fault and indeed this is the main reason I wrote this book! Second, they tend to misdiagnose the problem by believing that it's a "women's issue" and third, they can't find the time, energy or inclination, given their very busy lives. But unless women act, nothing will change.

The reason most women do not "see" lack of equality is because we don't think it impacts us directly. We convince ourselves that things aren't that bad. We see lots of women who suffer from violence, we see harassment every day and we see our sisters experiencing the difficult aftermath of divorce. However, we do not realize that all of these things are related to women's lack of influence and power.

Law Professor Deborah Rhodes describes the problem in this way, "A central problem for American women is the lack of consensus that there is a significant problem. Gender inequalities in leadership opportunities are pervasive; perceptions of inequality are not. A widespread assumption is that barriers have been coming down, women have been moving up and equal treatment is an accomplished fact. ... Such views are hard to square with the facts."

This is very important because unless women think there is a problem, we are unlikely to do anything about it. By not realizing that our personal problems are shared by millions of women we are less inclined to act. Yet by not speaking up we are inadvertently accepting the outcomes that include depression, stress and domestic upheaval and violence. These are all caused by the same thing. As a result women do what they can by volunteering for underfunded groups that, like triage in the emergency ward of a hospital, are just trying to stop the bleeding – for a while.

Another reason women do not "see" inequality is because there is almost no information about it. For myself, it took 20 years to fully understand what was really going on because so little is written, researched or published solely about the reality of women's lives and struggles. Other than a handful of academic treatises, there are few books addressing gender inequality head on that are geared to inform the general population about the issue. I found one book on raising children in a gender-neutral way and most of the books on equality or "breaking the glass ceiling" are lengthy treatises written by journalists who use a story-telling style that I found lacks flat-out practical advice.

As a society we don't know enough about women's full lives: Where women live and work, what they are doing in their homes, how they are contributing as paid workers, caregivers and volunteers. We don't know how friendships help women, how often women get depressed after having children or how much they pay for psycho-therapy after being pushed off the corporate ladder.

Although many scholars have dedicated their careers to the topic of women, relative to other topics, this research is just a drop in the bucket and rarely makes its way to the popular press (often because it is not always good news). The budget for research on women that is conducted at universities, mostly in sociology departments, is like a drop in the ocean compared to the budgets of medicine and engi-neering facilities. Indeed, we know way more about cancer than female depression and more about stocks and bonds than about the increases in our economy and overall happiness that would result if all mothers could work at high-paying, part-time jobs.

There are a handful of organizations who work at advancing women and promoting equality at a policy level. These include Catalyst, NOW (the National Organization of Women) and Ms Foundation, but most of these rely on private funding from individuals who wish to donate to stop inequality. These organizations are barely surviv-ing and not sustainable without significant sponsorship. Governments and corporations as a rule tend to turn a blind eye to inequality – one wonders if it is in the hope that women will remain ignorant and not complain.

As a result, there are very few people who know about the real causes of women's problems today and very few who are interested in educating women about these causes. If you look at the many women's networking groups and conferences you might be sur-prised to see that almost none of them talk about inequality. Women tend to not criticize things like corporate hierarchies when they actually benefit from the system. On the odd occasion, a speaker from Catalyst will attend a women's seminar and list all the depressing statistics on women's lack of advancement, which simply leaves women with no clear sense of what the real problem is (power) or how to make long-lasting changes.

Sadly, a recent article in the *Financial Post*, a Canadian national newspaper, suggested we dismantle all the current women's studies programs in colleges and universities, declaring (without any supporting evidence) that research on women and girls was neither necessary nor useful.

To compound such rhetoric, there is a sea of propaganda out there that tells us that women *do* have power and that everything is fine. All has been rectified. We're told that if we don't believe that, well then the problem must be in our own heads; that it's our "bad attitude," our "lack of courage" to "man up" and push ourselves forward or our "inability to keep things in balance" that should be examined.

The media tries to convince us that women are doing just fine, that a few women are even leading corporations and isn't that a wonderful thing? This alone leads many to believe that we no longer need to push for women's rights. We're told that women have achieved equality and are happy as clams, or at least "should be" happy (not to mention "thankful" that things aren't worse). The bottom line is that if there's no problem, then there's no conversation necessary and women don't need to speak up.

All this propaganda reinforces our fear of speaking out, which I describe in my book, *Lean Out*:

> We like to believe that women are powerful, even though the evidence says otherwise. Although women are barely advancing and are in many ways slipping back, women often stay silent – for three reasons. We prefer to stay positive and believe that things aren't that bad; we fear conflict or making a ruckus and we are ambivalent to powerful women. Our desire to ignore the problem is encouraged by a billion-dollar media industry that replaces our angst with

materialism – selling beauty and fashion while hiding the harsh reality of the majority of women. This opium, plus our fear of rocking the boat, keeps women passive and prevents us from participating in long-term improvements to women's lives. It also feeds our deeply held thoughts that perhaps women don't want or deserve power. Maybe women weren't meant to be powerful.

This method of silencing, however, comes at a cost to women and eventually filters down to children and families. Sue Monk Kidd describes the consequence of silencing women: "[Women] give themselves away. To avoid causing pain or inconvenience to others, they swallow their own needs and feelings. This loss of voice turns into resentment, eating disorders, rage, depression, low self-esteem, dependency and sexual dysfunction. They learn to be manipulative, indirect and passive to get what they need."

The Bottom Line. Most women do not see the extent of or full impact of female-male inequality. We know that women get paid less than men, and that they suffer from sexism and discrimination, but we don't see these as being a particularly big problem. We can't really see the problem, we misdiagnose the problem by thinking it's a "women's issue" and we can't find the time or energy to act. There are few books on the subject, almost nothing in popular magazines and barely any academic research on women's lives. And the propaganda machine keeps women ignorant and silent. This silence not only prevents change but eats women up from the inside.

What To Do. We must wake women up. We must gather the stories of women who feel the pain even if they do not know why. We must create an Occupy Women movement. This means educating women about what is really going on, getting them angry and mobilizing them in a way that will help them place pressure on the systems and barriers that are holding them back. We must look critically at the ways in which women are silenced and provide more supports for women who speak out.

As Marianne Williamson says, "Women are not powerless. We just pretend to be. We do this to a large part because we are afraid of the punishment inflicted on us when we dare to be who we really are. It's a subtle form of discrimination, but it's clearly there. A few women are allowed into the club, it seems: women who have allowed themselves to be partially declawed, their sexual threat to the status quo diminished just enough, so that men and women alike can handle the juice. But an animal in the wild is a beautiful thing."

Chapter 20

Help Women Be Small "p" and Big "P" Political

"Electing women to positions of political power does not in itself guarantee the expression of the feminine voice in the external world. Once in power, women can be tempted to conspire with the paternalistic system that they feel has so magnanimously allowed them a place at the table. They feel compelled to be strong men among strong men." ~ Marianne Williamson

Joke: Two men are talking to each other. The first man says, "Those Feminists are full of crap. We men should form a group of men just like them." The second man responds, "We did. It's called government."

As a society we have been slow to allow many groups access to power. Those with power, rarely handed it over. Our history is filled with stories of struggle from disenfranchised groups trying to claim their proper place. We have had thousands of wars that have seen the powerful slaughtering the less powerful, particularly if they had the gall to request access to power. In some instances, the less powerful were able to turn things around, but it's never easy. During the suffrage movement millions of women had to demonstrate, rally, petition and engage in a continuous fight for over a hundred years to get the vote. In the process women were outcast, shamed and even imprisoned for violating the law that they had no part in creating.

The truth is not pretty. When gross power imbalances exist, those in power tend to take advantage. Not only do many powerful groups disregard those who hold less power but they will often create mechanisms so that the power imbalance can be maintained in their favor.

Indeed Marianne Williamson sees the everyday treatment of women as an insidious attack on feminine power and the most emotionally violent and subversive force in our society today. She says, "Every time a women is raped, or beaten, every time a woman is attacked in the street or crucified in the press for no other reason than she is a woman, every time a strong woman is squeezed out of the workplace because her presence there is threatening to the older order – we are witnessing the skirmishes of a vast invisible war."

So what can women do? If women really want to see change come about they need to do three things:

- We must recognize the extent of the problem of inequality and must stop blaming ourselves or men and start focusing on the whole system and its many barriers that hold us back.

- We must focus on the deepest roots of the problem, not just the branches of the tree. This means examining the beliefs, institutions and tools that are holding women back

- We must take action if we truly want significant and long-lasting change. It can be small action or big action, but it must be action.

In the Introduction to this book I suggested that a small group of men control most of the world, politics, money and media. They also maintain their control by keeping others out of power, and specifically women. Then I asked: Who gave them this power? And who built the political system, the economic system and the corporate laws that allow them to do this?

If we use the metaphor of a playground to describe our current situation, how can we change the sandbox, the slide, the swings and the very way we play together?

In other words: How can we change the system from within as opposed to building our own brand new "female-friendly" playground? This means engaging from the top through our political system as well as working in a small "p" political way through grass roots movements.

Either way, the aim is to change the biases, laws, policies, rules and institutions that hold women back. Unless women change the rules of our society, we will continue to be controlled by those rules. Whether it's in kitchens, cafes, courtrooms or community centers, women must work together to bring about change because it's not likely going to happen on its own.

As for big "P" politics, women are severely lagging behind. There are only a few elected women in politics even in this day and age, but also few women in the backrooms who are informing changes to the laws and government policy. The whole political process is problem-atic for women – from elections to working in day-to day government. The general climate seems to be one of fighting and arguing and thus the person who is most attracted to this arena must be hard-nosed, power-hungry and even corrupt. Women's natural inclination is not to behave in this way, nor to operate in a system that promotes this kind of behavior.

Another barrier to politics for women is the practice and necessity of leaving one's family. This is not something that women, most par-ticularly women with small children, are prone to do. And if they do choose to take this route, there's still a stigma attached to a woman leaving her kids behind to pursue politics.

Not so for men; it's almost expected, and society is set up in such a way that most men have wives who are already the primary care-givers for their children. Stepping away from family for work has less consequence for men. The political process we have designed squeezes women out by requiring many out of town meetings, evening events and a high degree of travel. As well, the political fo-rum is one that is particularly hard on women. It is adversarial in that it requires competitive behavior, mud-slinging and winning over your opponents at all cost.

As for small "p" politics, women are masters of getting things done. However, one thing that stands in their way is fear. Have you ever wondered why there are not more feminists? Have you ever wondered why women are not more vocal considering they have been treated so badly and unfairly for centuries? As suggested above, one of the ways we keep women powerless is by silencing them. We tell women that to speak out is not only un-feminine but will cause them to be rejected by society. In extreme instances, it can even get them killed. Unfortunately, there are examples in history of women who spoke out and actually got their heads chopped off.

In spite of being fearful of speaking out, women must learn to believe in themselves and in their voice. As Williamson says, "We will not be free until we can speak our minds and our hearts without having to worry that men will crucify us, women will crucify us, the press will crucify us, or our children will be ashamed."

In her book, *Dance of the Dissident Daughter*, Sue Monk Kidd writes:

> With men at the top (or at least with a sense of entitlement about being at the top) and women below (or at least with a sense of belonging below) a way of relating was put in place based on dominance and dependence. The role, of the one above was to dominate and oversee the ones below. The role of the ones below was to answer to and depend on the one above. In addition, the one above learned how to protect his prestigious place on the top. He learned to stay up by keeping her down, that is, by insisting that she be content with the way things are.

Today the message to be both content and silent is more subtle, yet no less powerful. Women who speak out are still often silenced and shamed and thereby "put in their place."

Monk Kidd retells the Greek myth of Philomena, a woman who was raped and silenced. She writes:

The myth is about the loss of women's voices. It suggests that the source of female silence is the rape of the feminine – the devaluation and violation of femaleness. It suggests that when women protest this violation their voices are frequently squelched through ridicule, sanction and fear of reprisal. In the public arena, at church, work and home, women's tongues are often silenced when we dare to speak out our anger, truths and visions.

In my opinion, we women need desperately to heal from this ancient wound and can best act when grounded in our deepest feminine essence. Until we heal, we are simply fighting back with only part of ourselves.

The Bottom Line. If women really want to bring about change they must take action. This usually means getting political, either at the grass roots level or at higher levels in corporations and governments. This is the main way women can address the deepest issues relating to our societal culture, its rules and our institutions in which we work. This means either working in a small "p" or big "P" political way and getting elected to government or more locally engaging in small actions in the community or with women's groups. Right now, the political process is hostile to women and, as a result, few women run for office or get elected. *Silence* – it's not golden!

What To Do. We need to help women take political action, whether on the ground level or at the highest levels in organizations and movements. We need to find out what is holding women back and remove these barriers so that more women not only get elected, but are included in the law-making process. When looking at the political system we should question why it requires a lot of travel and odd hours of work and whether it needs to be so competitive and downright aggressive in the political arena of interaction. We need to support and work with organizations that gather research on social justice and equality issues, and turn this process around.

Chapter 21

Imagine Women as True Partners

"A truly equal world would be one where women ran half our countries and companies and men ran half our homes." ~ Sheryl Sandberg

This strategy of envisioning women and men as true partners is a very important one. This is because the task of creating a powerful new vision can motivate change. A vision provides a picture or shared dream of a better future. It describes a new way of being together and tells a new story about who we are as humans and how we can treat each other. A vision is not only inspiring, it provides a clear sense of direction and can also show us the steps we need to take to reach this common goal.

Salmon Rushdie describes it this way:

> We tell ourselves into being, don't we? ... I think that is one of the great reasons for stories. I mean, we are the storytelling animal, there is no other creature on earth that tells itself stories in order to understand who it is. This is what we do, we've always done it, whether they are religious stories or personal stories, or tall stories, or lies, or useful stories, we live by telling each other and telling ourselves the stories of ourselves. (Salman Rushdie in an interview with Britain's conservative magazine, *The Spectator*.)

At the beginning of this book I suggested that the best way to dismantle a patriarchal societal operating system is to look at each of its components as indicated in the following chart. This is so for re-visioning a new system.

There are two ways to envision a new reality. One is from the top down by envisioning what this world might look like in a utopian state. The other is to look at each of the three parts of the system (beliefs, institutions and tools of implementation) and consider ways to shift them individually. I think it's possible to do both things at the same time.

The RESULTS on Women (e.g., sexism and violence)		
Our BELIEFS about women (e.g., women should raise children)	Our INSTITUTIONS and policies (e.g., corporate hiring policies)	Our TOOLS of Implementation (e.g., TV, religious customs)

When building a new system the model might be better represented in the following way, as a straight line:

Beliefs $\Rightarrow$ Institutions $\Rightarrow$ Tools $\Rightarrow$ Results

It would be my preference to start with beliefs since I think that even the smallest changes to beliefs can have a huge ripple effect. A mind-set or thought is like a lever in terms of its impact on the whole system.

Indeed, as the bulk of *Occupy Women* has made clear, our outdated beliefs about women are at the root of all of the problems women face. Our ideas about what women can and should do have kept women out of high-paying jobs and politics and our ideas about how they should relate to others has left many subservient. Underlying these beliefs about women is what I call the "master belief" – that women are inferior to males or "not quite good enough." Here is a list of the top beliefs that I think can bring in a new world for women.

- **Women are valuable.** A first critical step therefore is to shift this idea and admit that women are not only valuable but of equal importance to men. As Selma Greenberg writes, "Not until Susan B. Anthony made her famous attempt to vote and was arrested did it become clear that some women might be uncouth enough to believe that they had been included in the phrase, 'All men are created equal'." Females are not second-class citizens.

- **The work that women do is valuable.** We need to see the work of women as being crucially important to society. As author Monk Kidd puts it, "In my wilder moments I imagined a society that paid child care workers, teachers, homeless advocates, poets, and bird watchers as much as it paid professional football players, generals and corporate CEOs. I tried to imagine a church where it mattered less what your beliefs and practices were and more how relationships were nurtured and healed."

- **Feminine traits are valuable.** We need to see so-called feminine skills or strengths like empathy and caring as not only important, but also belonging to both males and females. As Riane Eisler writes, "It's a peculiarly dominator way of thinking that labels empathy, caring and support as feminine traits. Both men and women have these abilities. And in partnership organization men are more apt to feel comfortable expressing them."

- **Women don't need to be controlled.** We no longer need to think that all women need male protection. In modern society it is condescending to think that an adult woman needs to be controlled, directed or protected by a male. If women have their own means of livelihood and equal access to opportunities, they will no longer need to depend on males for resources. As author Greenberg explains:

The bargain is acceptable to women only when they are trained from infancy to believe that their only hope for survival in a dangerous and fierce world is to gain the protection and support of one man. What happens then when girls and women come to believe that the exchange is no longer necessary? What happens when girls and women believe they can take care of themselves? The females may demand a more equal exchange.

If these new beliefs fly in the face of our outdated customs or traditions, we may be forced to reject one for the other. As Stephanie Vermeulen says: "Tradition is always difficult to tackle, because it's seen to be sacred. Tradition pretends to define what is right and wrong but in all societies the reality is relatively simple: tradition is used as the most powerful excuse to continue to unconsciously conserve male power. So how much longer are we women going to humor tradition by forfeiting our health and our happiness?"

I remember being at a family party years ago when a very angry grandmother approached me and accused me of ruining the lives of all women because I had suggested that when women allowed men to open their doors, women were remaining in the "dependency exchange" whereby men offered chivalry or protection in order to be put on a pedestal. By doing this women were expected to be appreciative of their protectors. As a friend of mine used to say, "A gift that comes with expectations is no gift at all."

At the same time as shifting our beliefs, we can also revise our institutions. Riane Eisler suggests that because our systems were built on these outdated thoughts, they too reflect a power imbalance that she refers to as "hierarchies of domination." From corporations to families most of our systems are designed to keep the power at the top – through the use of dominance. If we look at some of the systems, what we need to do seems obvious.

- Economic system → pay women fairly and value women's work.

- Judicial system → ensure women are engaged in all parts of the system.

- Family system → ensure all family members are treated fairly and equitably.

- Corporate system → remove all barriers for women, mentor them and provide supports.

- Political system → ensure women have influence in elections and governance.

- Education system → ensure women are represented at all levels from preschool to university.

Dr. Eisler suggests a type of "partnership model" where people are partners, rather than owners and workers or breadwinners and homemakers. Within this system she recommends adopting "hierarchies of actualization" where leaders or fathers are not dominators, but side-by-side guides. These structures empower rather than disempower others. People would act as mentors and facilitators, not police officers or controllers. These types of structures could be more flexible and result in better communication and an improved way of tapping each person's knowledge and skills.

Similarly, in her book, *The Female Advantage*, Sally Helgesen refers to a preferable way for people to work together as "webs of inclusion" as opposed to hierarchies of exclusion. These webs permit greater flow of information and thus tend to be more successful.

As for a new vision, it is also important to focus on more positive relationships between people. In my opinion, one of the most devastating impacts of a patriarchal world is the harm caused to all relationships and particularly husband-wife and women's friendships. Indeed

Greenberg suggests that when women are equal and have equal opportunity, the traditional relationship between men and women will dissolve. The bargain that women have been encouraged to accept for so long – male support and protection in exchange for female love, sex and service – will not survive.

As Marianne Williamson says, we must relinquish the paradigm of men as power with women as support and instead embrace the image of both men and women as powerful, each supporting each other. "A woman has a mighty and sacred task to perform on earth. She will not be able to function if she remains with a man who derides her glory." She goes on to say, "A secure man is not threatened by a women's intellectual or emotional power but celebrates the opportunity for joyful partnership that it offers."

I often hear women bemoaning the fact that women are their "worst enemies" or, worse yet, are not to be trusted. Not only is this a terrible loss to women who benefit enormously from women companions, but it also causes women to silence each other, as described here by Williamson:

> Every time a woman at a dinner party fails to support another woman who dares to express herself with pure emotion and power, she is betraying the Goddess. And why? Don't miss this girls. Because at the deepest levels, we're afraid we won't be attractive to the men at the table if we dare to voice our hearts. We're afraid we won't be as sexy as we would be if we just sat there and played china doll, making no waves, threatening no man.

In this new vision, women and men would share power, neither being a threat to either – as a result both could flourish.

Sheila Ellison collected a list of ideas about what an ideal world might look like in her book, *If Women Ruled the World.* Her list included ideas such as:

- We'd form a society based on partnership.

- Women's voices would be heard.

- Women would not give their power away.

- We'd learn to disappoint others.

- We would love our thighs.

- We would be sexual dynamos.

- We'd speak the truth even in difficult situations.

- Business would be more fun.

- We would portray real women in advertisements.

But to change our system and all its components we need all women to speak up, not just those in influential positions of public policy-making or those who enjoy advocating for women rights.

We need women who believe in equality all the way from the "bottom to the top." We need women whose life experiences parallel our own. This is the only way we can fill the huge differences in opinion in the legislatures about issues that impact women – issues like education, children, the environment and health care.

The Bottom Line. If we truly want women and all people to thrive and contribute to society, we must first admit that our society is not functioning very well. We must look at everything as an anthropologist would, and notice how they are preventing women and men from flourishing together. As for our beliefs, we can choose to think in a more open-minded way. We do not have to hold onto thoughts simply because our parents did or because it is based on tradition. We can create a vision of society where women and men are true partners.

What To Do. In order to bring about a brand new system we need to do two things: create a fresh vision of "utopia" and also work at shifting the individual parts of our current system, namely our beliefs, institutions and tools. As for beliefs, the most important are as follows: We must believe that women are valuable, that the work women do is valuable, that feminine traits are valuable and that women don't need to be controlled. As well, we need to look at each of our institutions with a critical eye, from our economic and corporate systems to our family and religious institutions. Do they reflect our modern beliefs and modern society? We must commit to building true partnerships rather than hierarchies or top-down, dominance-based relationships. Instead of "one-upmanship" our connections would look like continuously growing webs of inclusion.

In an ideal world, our institutions would not only allow for the tapping of everyone's strengths, but would permit continuous evolution of both individuals and the systems themselves. They would better accommodate not only our human needs, but the needs of the whole planet. In an ultimate utopian environment, these systems would take into account the natural rhythms of our bodies and of nature and in doing so we could promote a sustainable future together.

Conclusion

"We have the opportunity to forge a marriage between the masculine and the feminine, more potent and more vibrant than any we have experienced on the earth for ages – more beautiful perhaps than any the earth has ever known." ~ Marianne Williamson

In this book I invite both men and women to create a movement. And the first step in any movement is to speak "truth to power." This means you must tell the truth even if you have no power in the current system and you take the risk that those who have power are not going to like what you have to say. It's like telling the emperor he has no clothes.

This is precisely what *Occupy Women* does and this is exactly the risk I am willing to take. If not me, then who?

I believe that if we allow women access to more power, our whole world would change overnight. The lives of women would improve, our systems would function better and our society would benefit in ways we never dreamed of. I also believe that the root to all women's lack of power is our currently accepted society-wide "operating system."

This book shows how our this system harms both women and our whole society and goes by several names. Whether call it "patriarchy," "The White Male System" or a "Dominance-Based System," it provides a blueprint for the operation of our society and in many ways holds women back.

First, it deems the world one big hierarchy with men at the top. It also believes in the use of force or dominance to maintain control and it treats women as second-class citizens. At its core is the idea that males are more valuable that females, that masculine traits are preferable to feminine traits and that men's work is more valuable than women's. It also sees the role of women in society to be secondary to men with their primary role as supporting men.

This system that sets out the laws and rules by which our whole society operates is no longer a good fit with the realities of today's society. Still it goes unchallenged because it is largely invisible and is accepted as the status quo. Indeed the system is designed to keep those at the top in control and in power. As well, those who oppose the system, such as women, are silenced by propaganda, rhetoric and direct attacks.

For almost 100 years, suffragists and feminists fought hard against this system and were able to make some strides, including the right to vote, the right to work and the right to own property. Still the system chugs along with many of our outdated beliefs flourishing and dominance-based institutions thriving.

Luckily, many women are waking up and taking action. With the recent popularity of the word "feminism," women are realizing they can finally speak openly about their lives.

So what is the solution? Three things:

- We must acknowledge women's reality and see the link between "women's problems" (such a violence, poverty and discrimination) and our patriarchal system. We must refrain from blaming men, women, cultures or religions and instead blame the whole system. We must never be afraid to use the word "patriarchy."

- We must look at the various parts of this system and how they work together to keep women down. This includes the *beliefs* we have about women, the *institutions* built upon these beliefs and the *tools* we use to implement and reinforce these institutions.

- We must take action. Talking about it is not enough. We must stop asking women to do all the heavy lifting and work together as partners at building a new society based on principles of inclusion and equality. Men and women together.

After all is said and done, perhaps the most important thing we can do as individuals is to believe. To believe that things can be better and that we can be full partners in creating a better world.

Most importantly I want to remind all women:

- You are perfect just as you are and should never feel like you are not good enough.

- Although you are currently being treated poorly and unfairly, as human beings, you deserve so much more. Any culture that does not fully appreciate women is wrong.

- You are not alone. Millions of women all over the world feel just as you do.

I believe we are at a turning point and that things are on the cusp of changing significantly. With books like this and the voices and writings of many women (on whose shoulders I stand) we can together (with men) make this world a better place for everyone.

If you really want to bring about equality for women the first step is easy. Simply share what you have learned in this book. Give this book to your sister, a friend, your niece or daughter. Share the 21 strategies at the end of this book (*Occupy Women – A Manifesto for Equality*). Copy the list and distribute it widely or share it on social media (contact the author for an electronic version). Talk to others and have gatherings.

If not now, when? If not you, then who?

"I think they [women] are our hope, we men have made a mess and we ought to get out of the way and let women who are truly feminine take over." ~ Archbishop Desmond Tutu, World Social Forum 2007

21 Strategies

1. Acknowledge our thousand-year-old hierarchy
2. Uncover our hidden cultural rules
3. Challenge male privilege
4. Balance masculine and feminine
5. Question the "Femininity Message"
6. End the media's stereotyping
7. Don't expect women to be beauty models
8. Eradicate pornography and the sexualization of women and girls
9. Challenge the tyranny of niceness
10. Value the intelligence of emotions
11. Remember women's history
12. Explore our fear of strong women
13. See the link between power and violence
14. Ensure women participate in daily news
15. Understand what true equality means
16. Embrace divine feminine power
17. Engage men and boys
18. Use language that includes women
19. Create an Occupy Women Movement
20. Help women be small "p" and big "P" political
21. Imagine women as true partners

Selected Bibliography

Babcock, Linda and Sara Laschever. *Women Don't Ask: The High Cost of Avoiding Negotiation – and Strategies for Change.* Bantam Dell, 2007.

Bennetts, Leslie. *The Feminine Mistake: Are We Giving Up Too Much?* Hyperion, 2007.

Carter, Jimmy. *A Call to Action: Women, Religion, Violence and Power.* Simon Schuster, 2014.

de Beauvoir, Simone. *The Second Sex.* Knopf, 1953.

Dee, Catherine. *A Girls' Guide to Life: Take Charge of Your Personal Life, Your School Time, Your Social Scene, and Much More!* Little Brown, 2005.

Dolan-Del Vecchio, Ken. *Making Love, Playing Power: Men, Women and the Rewards of Intimate Justice.* Soft Skull Press, 2008.

Douglas, Susan J. and Meredith W. Michaels. *The Mommy Myth: The Idealization of Motherhood and How It Has Undermined All Women.* Free Press, 2004.

Eisler, Riane. *The Chalice and the Blade: Our History, Our Future.* Harper San Francisco, 1988.

— —. *The Power of Partnership: Seven Relationships that Will Change Your Life.* New World Library, 2002.

— —. *The Real Wealth of Nations: Creating a Caring Economics.* Berrett-Koehler, 2007.

Ellison, Sheila (ed.) and Marie Wilson. *If Women Ruled the World: How to Create the World We Want to Live In.* New World Library, 2004.

Elium, Jeanne and Don Elium. *Raising a Daughter: Parents and the Awakening of a Healthy Woman.* Celestial Arts, 2003.

Ensler, Eve. *The Vagina Monologues.* Dramatist's Play Service, 2000.

Evans, Gail. *She Wins, You Win: The Most Important Rule Every Business Woman Needs to Know.* Gotham, 2003.

Faludi, Susan. *Backlash: The Undeclared War Against American Women.* Anchor, 1992.

Fisher, Helen. *The First Sex: The Natural Talents of Women and How They are Changing the World.* Random House, 1999.

Fitzgerald, Maureen. *Lean Out: How to Dismantle the Corporate Barriers that Hold Women Back.* Centerpoint Media, 2016.

— —. *Motherhood is Madness: How to Break the Chains that Prevent Mothers from Being Truly Happy.* Centerpoint Media, 2015.

French, Marilyn. *The War Against Women.* Ballantine Books, 1992.

— —. *Beyond Power: On Women, Men and Morals.* Ballantine Books, 1985.

Friedan, Betty. *The Feminine Mystique.* Norton, 1963.

Greenberg, Selma. *Right from the Start: A Guide to Non-Sexist Child Rearing.* Houghton Mifflin, 1979.

Helgesen, Sally. *The Female Advantage: Women's Way of Leadership.* Currency Doubleday, 1990.

Hewlett, Sylvia A. *Off Ramps and On Ramps: Keeping Talented Women on the Road to Success.* Harvard Business Review Press, 2007.

— — and Cornel West. *The War Against Parents: What We Can Do for America's Beleaguered Moms and Dads*. Houghton Mifflin, 1998.

Hochschild, Arlie R. and Anne Machung. *The Second Shift*. Penguin, 2003.

Katz, Jackson. *Tough Guise: Violence, Media, and the Crisis in Masculinity*. (Documentary) Media Education Foundation, 1999.

Kellerman, Barbara and Deborah Rhode. *Women and Leadership: The State of Play and Strategies for Change.* Jossey-Bass, 2007.

Kidd, Sue Monk. *Dance of the Dissident Daughter: A Women's Journey from Christian Tradition to the Sacred Feminine*. Harper, 1996.

Kilbourne, Jean. *See* Lazarus, Margaret.

Kristof, Nicholas, and Sheryl WuDunn. *Half the Sky: Turning Oppression into Opportunity for Women Worldwide*. Knopf, 2009.

Kunin, Madeline. *The New Feminist Agenda: Defining the Next Revolution for Women, Work, and Family.* Chelsea Green Publishing, 2012.

Lamb, Sharon and Lyn Mikel Brown. *Packaging Girlhood: Rescuing Our Daughters from Marketer's Schemes.* St Martins Griffin, 2006.

Lazarus, Margaret, Renner Wunderlich, Patricia Stallone, and Joseph Vitagliano. *Killing Us Softly: Advertising's Image of Women.* Cambridge Documentary Films, Inc., 1979. Based on a lecture by Jean Kilbourne.

Marone, Nicky. *How to Mother a Successful Daughter: A Practical Guide to Empowering Girls from Birth to Eighteen.* Harmony, 1998.

Meyerson, Deborah and Robin Ely. "Using Difference to Make a Difference" in *The Difference "Difference" Makes: Women and Leadership*, edited by Deborah Rhode. Stanford University Press, 2003.

Miles, Rosalind. *Who Cooked the Last Super: The Women's History of the World*. Broadway Books, 2001.

Miller, Jean Baker. *Toward a New Psychology of Women*. Beacon Press, 1987.

Moen, Phyllis and Patricia Roehling. *Career Mystique: Cracks in the American Dream*. Rowman and Littlefield, 2004.

Newsom, Jennifer Siebel. *MISSRepresentation*. (Documentary) Girls Club Entertainment, 2011.

O'Reilly, Andrea. *Mother Outlaws: Theories and Practices of Empowered Mothering*. Women's Press, 2004.

Pipher, Mary. *Reviving Ophelia: Saving the Selves of Adolescent Girls*. Ballantine, 1994.

Rich, Adrienne. *Of Woman Born: Motherhood as Experience and Institution*. W.W. Norton, 1986.

Roberts, Anita. *Safe Teens: Powerful Alternatives to Violence*. Polestar Books, 2001.

Sandberg, Sheryl. *Lean In: Women, Work and the Will to Lead*. Knopf, 2013.

Schaef, Anne Wilson. *Meditations for Women Who Do Too Much*. Harper Collins, 1990.

— —. *Women's Reality: An Emerging Female System in a White Male Society*. Harper & Row, 1981.

Shalit, Wendy. *Girls Gone Mild: Young Women Reclaim Self-Respect and Find It's Not Bad to be Good*. Random House, 2007.

Shipman, Claire and Katty Kay. *Womenomics: Write Your Own Rules for Success*. Harper, 2009.

Silverstein, Brett and Deborah Perlick. *The Cost of Competence: Why Inequality Causes Depression, Eating Disorders and Illness in Women.* Oxford University Press, 1995.

Slaughter, Anne-Marie. "Why Women Can't Have it All." *Atlantic,* July-August 2012, (thealtantic.com/magazine/archive/2012/07/).

Smith, Dayle M. *Women at Work: Leadership for the Next Century.* Prentice Hall, 1999.

Solovic, Susan. *The Girls' Guide to Power and Success.* Amacom, 2001.

Stone, Pamela. *Opting Out? Why Women Really Quit Careers and Head Home.* University of California Press, 2007.

Stone, Sidra. *The Shadow King: The Invisible Force that Holds Women Back.* iUniverse, 1997.

Tannen, Deborah. *You Don't Understand: Women and Men in Conversation.* William Morrow, 2007.

— —. *Talking from 9-5: Women and Men at Work.* Quill, 1994.

The Conference Board of Canada. *Women on Boards: Not Just the Right Thing...But the "Bright" Thing.* The Conference Board of Canada, 2002.

Valenti, Jessica. *He's a Stud, She's a Slut and 49 Other Double Standards Every Woman Should Know.* Seal Press, 2008.

Vermeulen, Stephanie. *Stitched Up: Who Fashions Women's Lives?* Jacana, 2005.

Warner, Judith. *Perfect Madness: Motherhood in the Age of Anxiety.* Riverhead, 2005.

Williams, Joan C. and Rachel Demspey. *What Women Want at Work: Four Patterns Working Women Need to Know.* New York University Press, 2014.

Williamson, Marianne. *A Woman's Worth*. Ballantine, 1994.

Wolf, Naomi. *The Beauty Myth: How Images of Beauty Are Used Against Women*. Doubleday, 1991.

Zhao, Xiaolan. *Reflections of the Moon on Water: Healing Women's Bodies and Minds through Traditional Chinese Wisdom*. Vintage Canada Edition, 2006.

Acknowledgements

Occupy Women really began about ten years ago on the day I bought Anne Wilson Schaef's book in my neighborhood used book store. After reading *Women's Reality: An Emerging Female System in a White Male Society* I was able to trust myself to share what I have come to know over my entire life. Although I have never met Anne, she is obviously an extraordinarily brilliant and wise woman. I keep her little book, *Meditations for Women Who Do Too Much,* on my bedside table.

I also wish to I acknowledge the hundreds (perhaps thousands) of women who have taught me so very much on this journey. Although they do not know it, they have saved my life. Here are the writers who have influenced me most:

- Marianne Williamson, *A Woman's Worth*

- Sue Monk Kidd, *Dance of the Dissident Daughter*

- Riane Eisler, *The Power of Partnership* and *The Chalice and the Blade*

- Marilyn French, *The War Against Women*

- Judith Warner, *Perfect Madness*

I also want to thank all of those amazing women who helped on this book and in particular Nance Fleming who added a whole new brilliance to what I was trying desperately to put into compassionate wording! I also truly appreciate Catherine Leek, Karin Mizgala, Sandra Herd, Monica Beauregard, Mary-Jean Payeur, Mary Pappajohn, Christine Dearing, Denise Withers, Jennifer Leslie, Christine Unterthiner, Susanne Doyle-Ingram and Darrell Tomkins. And Paul, of course.

About the Author

Maureen F. Fitzgerald, PhD, JD, LLM, BComm is a recovering lawyer, author and change agent. She practiced law for over 20 years and is the founder of CenterPoint Media, a multimedia publisher of books that advance thinking.

In her former life, Maureen was a labor lawyer, a policy lawyer and a mediator. She was also a professor of law at two universities and has written twelve books and many articles – both academic and practical. She has a business degree, two law degrees, a masters' degree in law from the London School of Economics and a doctorate degree in philosophy.

Always a leader of both people and ideas, Maureen speaks across North America about social justice, equality and mindfulness. Her motto is: *Sharing the right ideas at the right time can change the world.*

Maureen is the author of the following books:

- ***Lean Out****: How to Dismantle the Corporate Barriers that Hold Women Back.*

- ***Motherhood is Madness****: How to Break the Chains that Prevent Mothers from Being Truly Happy.*

- ***Occupy Women****: A Manifesto for Positive Change in a World Run by Men.*

- ***A Woman's Circle:*** *Create a Peer Mentoring Group for Advice, Networking, Support and Connection.*

- ***Invite the Bully to Tea:*** *End Harassment, Bullying and Dysfunction Forever with a Simple yet Radical New Approach.*

- ***If Not Now, When?*** *Create a Life and Career of Purpose with a Powerful Vision, a Mission Statement and Measurable Goals.*

- ***Mindfulness Made Easy:*** *50 Simple Practices to Reduce Stress, Create Calm and Live in the Moment – At Home, Work and School.*

- ***Hiring, Managing and Keeping the Best:*** *The Complete Canadian Guide for Employers,* with Monica Beauregard.

- ***So You Think You Need a Lawyer:*** *How to Screen, Hire, Manage or Fire a Lawyer.*

- ***Legal Problem Solving:*** *Reasoning, Research and Writing (7ed).* Lexis/Nexis.

- ***Wake up Sleeping Beauty****: Protect Your Daughter from Sexism, Stereotypes and Sexualization [2016].*

- ***Mean Girls Aren't Mean****: Stand up to Cliques, Bullies, Peer Pressure and Popularity and Empower Girls in a Radical New Way [2016].*

- ***Gritty Is the New Pretty:*** *Raise Confident, Courageous and Resilient Girls in a Man's World [2016].*

You can find her at www.MaureenFitzgerald.com.

Books in This Series

How to dismantle the corporate
barriers that hold women back

LEAN OUT

Maureen F. Fitzgerald, PhD

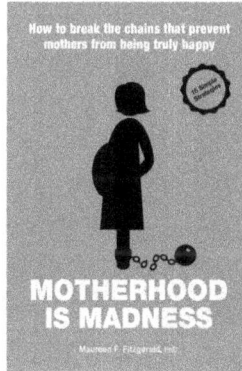

How to break the chains that prevent
mothers from being truly happy

MOTHERHOOD
IS MADNESS

Maureen F. Fitzgerald, PhD

A manifesto for positive change
in a world run by men

OCCUPY
WOMEN

Maureen F. Fitzgerald, PhD

www.ingramcontent.com/pod-product-compliance
Lightning Source LLC
Chambersburg PA
CBHW072133020426
42334CB00018B/1787